THE CLASSICAL AMERICAN HOUSE

THE CLASSICAL AMERICAN HOUSE

images
Publishing

Published in Australia in 2017 by
The Images Publishing Group Pty Ltd
ABN 89 059 734 431
6 Bastow Place, Mulgrave, Victoria 3170, Australia
Tel: +61 3 9561 5544 Fax: +61 3 9561 4860
books@imagespublishing.com
www.imagespublishing.com

Copyright © The Images Publishing Group Pty Ltd 2017
The Images Publishing Group Reference Number: 1240

National Library of Australia Cataloguing-in-Publication entry

Title: The Classical American House: The Classical Architecture Collection /
            Introduction by Phillip James Dodd.
ISBN: 9781864706826 (hardback)

Notes: Includes index.

Subjects: Architecture, Classical—United States.
            Architecture—United States.
            Architectural design—United States.

Production manager: Rod Gilbert
Senior editor: Gina Tsarouhas
Graphic designer: Nicole Boehringer

Printed on 150gsm Lumis Silk art paper by Everbest Printing Investment Limited, in Hong Kong/China

IMAGES has included on its website a page for special notices in relation to this and our other publications.
Please visit www.imagespublishing.com

CONTENTS

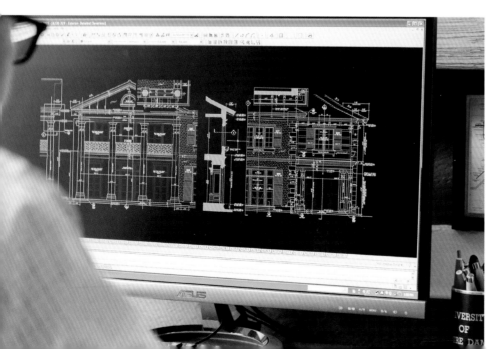

INTRODUCTION

The tradition of the classical house is not only alive and well, it is flourishing, perhaps no more so than in America. Our lives and our workplace may well be dominated by contemporary forms of sophisticated technology, but deep down for our homes we desire surroundings which are familiar, traditional, well-tried, and above all, beautiful. Such a desire does not mean that we are any less modern. On the contrary, we can still remain modern and up-to-date in terms of our technological approach to life, while at the same time satisfying the intangible needs of the spirit and a sense of place—as demonstrated by the beautiful contemporary classical homes shown in the following pages.

What is the *classical house* in the 21st century? For many, classical architecture denotes a form of design that looks back to the past—to the principles of ancient Greece and Rome, and their use of the five orders (Tuscan, Doric, Ionic, Corinthian, and Composite), each with their own rules of proportion and ornamentation. In particular, classical architects adhere to the writings of Vitruvius, Leon Battista Alberti, Andrea Palladio, Sebastiano Serlio, Giacomo Barozzi da Vignola, and their rules on architectural design. However, nowadays it is perhaps more appropriate to describe a building, specifically a house, as *classical* in conjuncture with the terms *traditional* and *vernacular*. A house's roots may well be found in classical antiquity, or perhaps via the Italian Renaissance or the English Georgian period, but its specific design has evolved over time to reflect the environmental, cultural, technological, economic, and historical context in which it exists. We look to the past to apply the lessons learnt from our forebears, but adapt those to better fit within a modern context.

Why is the *classical house* so popular in modern-day America? To the outside world, America—as a relatively new country—is seen as the epitome of the modern world, synonymous with innovation, and at the forefront of the great technological advancements of our times. One does not immediately conjure up the terms classical or traditional in describing this great nation, or indeed, its architecture. Yet when the founding fathers (and in particular Thomas Jefferson) aimed to affirm their newfound democratic independence via an architectural vocabulary, they chose to look to the past and emulate the architecture of ancient Greece and Rome. In turn, the Greek Revival style further referenced the architecture of ancient Athens, as it aimed to represent the ideals of patriotism and democracy that America strived for. Ever since then, the classical house in America has been closely associated with those same ideals—yet interestingly, without the negative associations of the class structure found in similar English and French classical houses.

In recent years we have also witnessed a backlash towards the globalization of the previous generation, where individual countries, cities, towns, villages, streets, and houses lost their sense of identity, and above all, their unique character. We have now learnt that by ignoring the past and our traditions, and by consistently denying their relevance to the present day, we have gradually eroded our architectural, cultural and political identities—that sense of civic pride, of belonging to a particular place, and of having roots. We have come again to realize that certain values and principles are eternal ones; that the character of our houses, which is so evident in the local architecture of each region, is part of a larger rich tradition that we've inherited from our forebears. Above all, our houses—our homes—characterize who we are; they portray who we are, or more accurately, the image of ourselves that we wish to portray.

Why are there so many differing styles of *classical house* in America? Well, architecture in America is as rich and diverse as its multicultural society, and as broad and vast as its enormous landscape. It represents a rich eclectic and innovative tradition that recognizes that its heritage came about as a result of a response to regional climatic conditions, the availability of certain local materials, and through the inspiration of the grander examples of European architecture. In other words: climate, materials, and tradition. These are the three primary influences that determine the specific architectural character of our houses, and what allows them to successfully blend into the historic fabric of our landscape.

These three primary influences, or orders, can be further characterized by Sir Henry Wotton in his volume of *The Elements of Architecture*. Published in 1624, it is the first translation of *de Architectura* by Vitruvius, and is the first to quote, "well building hath three conditions: firmness, commodity and delight."

For example, houses found in the colder northern parts of the country that suffer from large amounts of snow, will tend to have tall steeply pitched roofs to allow snow to slide off quickly and prevent it from accumulating. On the other hand, houses in warmer southern tropical regions will have a low pitched roof with a large overhang, to provide shade from the sun and aid in the detrimental effects of rainwater run-off during heavy storms. In either case, the particular function

of the roof starts to determine the shape, form, proportions, and eventually the style of the house. Despite all of the technological advancements available to use today, nothing provides shelter from the sun, rain and snow better than a traditionally designed roof—something that those of us with flat modern roofs can surely attest to. Function must always determine and trump aesthetics.

By using local materials, we ensure that our houses look as if they belong—that they have grown out of our architectural tradition and are in harmony with nature. Historically, North America and Europe were covered in expansive forests and rich foliage which inspired the construction of many timber-framed homes, often covered with clapboard siding for the walls and shingles for the roof. Gradually there developed a hierarchy of materials, with brick, stone and slate used to promote ones wealth and status in the local community—especially within the more prosperous settlements surrounding New York. But even then, these were materials quarried locally, or in the case of brick, by using clay from nearby, which would often result in a finished brick of a certain color specific to that area. As the nation expanded, and with the advent of the railroads, it became possible to easily transport building materials around the country. Stone quarried in Maine or Minnesota could now be used to adorn a building in New York City.

But perhaps the most important of the three primary influences in creating the design aesthetic of a particular region, are the traditions of its initial settlers, and the architectural vocabulary they choose. As an immigrant myself, I find that I surround myself with things to remind me of the country of my birth, as if trying to not lose ones identity. This was the same for the English, Dutch, German, and French who established the first North American colonies. They not only named their new towns and villages after the ones they had left (New Haven, New London and New York), they also brought with them knowledge of specific wood-framing and construction techniques.

Unsurprisingly during Colonial times, much of the architecture emulated that of the Georgian-era houses being built in England, but adapted to the fit an American context. Instead of using brick, wood was used in New England in

Previous pages (top) The design process, for this Spanish Mediterranean–style home in Palm Beach, starts with Phillip creating hand-drawn colored pencil sketches. Color is important as it helps determine material selection, as well as landscaping components that are an integral component of the overall architectural design. In the early design stages of a project, hand sketches are also more practical and relatable for presenting the overall concept to the homeowner. (bottom left) As the design develops, Phillip drafts up detailed elevations on the computer. It is important to note that the computer is used as a tool, just like a pencil, in recording the information required to construct the home and gain the necessary municipal approvals. (bottom right) Construction drawings are printed, and then checked using proportional dividers. Time is spent to compose the drawing to look like a traditionally hand-drafted sheet. This is not for aesthetic purposes, but more so in that it makes us carefully consider what is and what is not included on a drawing. It is that eye-to-brain-to-hand coordination that is missing when one relies on, and is dictated to, by the computer.

Opposite, above and following page Computer renderings of the new Spanish Mediterranean–style home designed by Phillip. Computer-generated perspectives like these, are instrumental in presenting a three-dimensional design to the homeowner, as flat traditional elevations can be very misleading. By showing landscaping, weathering the materials to show a patina, and adding shadows, the homeowner can easily see what their home will eventually look like.

what we now refer to as the Colonial style. In our cities, where fireproofing was desired, brick was used. In the Bahamas the same Georgian style was modified using local materials and employed deep porches and roof overhangs to shade from the sun, in what we now call Anglo-Caribbean or British Colonial style. Every state and every region can boast its own unique take on Georgian architecture, based upon the materials that were available, the craftsmanship of its builders, and the climate it had to guard against.

Further south—and west—we find the influences of Spanish and Mediterranean architecture in such settlements of St. Augustine in Florida, Santa Fe in New Mexico, and the California missions. The architecture of these early settlements, helped create the distinctly American Mediterranean Revival style which blended together references from Spanish Renaissance, Spanish Colonial, Beaux-Arts, Italian Renaissance, and Venetian Gothic architecture, to create coastal villas and resorts in California and Florida.

Along the Gulf Coast and in Louisiana, the area was settled by the French who developed the Creole style of architecture by blending together French Canadian and Caribbean architecture. Even after the Spanish assumed control of the region in 1763, they continued to build in this modified French style (most famously the French Quarter in New Orleans)—as by then its architectural vocabulary had created a unique sense of identity.

In our cities, we see an even broader variety of styles, matching the diversity of its population, the fashions of the time, and the wealth of its residents. In Manhattan we see brick Georgian townhouses being replaced by the more slender proportions of Victorian Italianate brownstones in the West Village. We have the Beaux-Arts mansions of Fifth Avenue, inspired by Italian Renaissance and Gothic Revival architecture; the Parisian inspired apartment buildings of the Upper West Side; and finally that distinctly American form of architecture—the skyscraper. This eclectic medley of styles fuses together perfectly in a way only found in American cities, as each represents a specific time in that city's evolution. In New York, during the Gilded Age, these architectural styles were carefully selected and curated to create an architectural history consummate with a new city aiming to revive the cultural capitals of Athens, London, Paris, and Rome.

The seven architectural firms that are featured in this book are all regional proponents of classical house design. Although their work differs greatly, they all practice with a deference to scale, harmony, and above all, character. Each embraces the regional influences of climate, materials, and tradition, to design houses that fit seamlessly and effortlessly into their local environment. Each of their designs has a clear sense of place that reflects the traditions of the generations that have come before us. Yet each is a contemporary house—not a period house—as they provide all of the creature comforts and technologies that we expect in our homes nowadays. Combined, their body of work is testament to the enduring eclectic architectural legacy of America; and testament that the tradition of the classical house in America is alive, well, and indeed prospering.

CHARLES HILTON ARCHITECTS

Rare is the affluent American enclave as storied, stylish, and sophisticated as Greenwich. Located just 30 miles (48 kilometers) northeast of Midtown Manhattan, from the shores of Connecticut's Gold Coast, this exclusive hamlet combines the peace and serenity of a pastoral small town with the culture and cachet of a bustling cosmopolitan center. It is home to some of the most superlative estates in the United States, and it continues to beckon titans of industry and financial magnates, as well as business-building entrepreneurs and creative types. They come today from all over the world, to immerse themselves in the refined luxury and timeless, understated good taste that Greenwich so uniquely embraces and embodies.

It is against this backdrop of style and sophistication that award-winning architect Charles Hilton has built his career, creating more than 250 exceptional residences in and around Greenwich over the course of three decades. Capitalizing on his broad and deep knowledge of the region's history of fine architecture, Hilton has established his eponymous firm as an expert authority. Whether meticulously designing a pitch-perfect Palladian villa or Country Georgian estate, a detail-rich European-style farmhouse or a Shingle Style beach house, Hilton sensitively weaves classical architecture with the substantial modern amenities his discerning clientele expects.

Hilton developed an early admiration for the vernacular residential styles of the Northeast. He brought this appreciation with him to design school, and although his education at

Pennsylvania State University and Germany's Technische Universitat in Darmstadt focused on modernism, his first job after college, in 1988, returned him to the classics. This postgraduate position is what brought him to Greenwich, and he's worked there ever since, establishing his first studio in 1991.

Like his clients, Hilton has an innate curiosity for culture and history, and, like those homeowners, he's willing to invest time, energy, and funds in thoughtful, meticulous work. He roots these residences in principles of traditional architecture that transcend time, style, and taste: human scale and proportion, historical relevance, honest materials, and quality craftsmanship, among them. Hilton excels at creating classical buildings that expertly accommodate contemporary lifestyles. They incorporate modern technology, and they reflect the diversity of the global society in which we now live. While many may appear entirely traditional on the outside, inside, they are designed for contemporary living. His homes are light filled, with plans that encourage natural flow, easy entertaining, playful family interactions, and indoor-outdoor living. They feature the sorts of spaces and amenities desired today, from mudrooms to great rooms, media centers to eat-in chef's kitchens, as well as smart-home technology, energy efficient systems, and environmentally sensitive materials.

Hilton has dedicated his career to creating imaginative, historically relevant buildings that inspire and delight, meaningfully improving the lives of their inhabitants.

"Built to last, his houses evoke history, import, and sophistication… these buildings
are not merely shelters or dwellings, but stage sets for exceptional living!"

Country Georgian Estate

Greenwich, Connecticut

If there is one classical aesthetic for which the firm is best known, it is Georgian Colonial. The style traces its roots to Renaissance Europe in the 15th century. Later, it made its way to England and, eventually, to colonial America. There it took root in such early settlements as Williamsburg, Virginia; Philadelphia; and Boston, before spreading up and down the East Coast during the Colonial Revival period in the early 20th century. Hilton finds the style particularly well suited to Greenwich. Its large, flat, and gently sloping parcels lend themselves to the symmetry and balance of these buildings, whose formal stature allows them to sit grandly on their acreages. The look uses a relatively simple palette of masonry walls and slate roofs, with white-painted wood and patinated copper details. Hilton's skill reveals itself through the combination of these elements and through a sense of proportion and scale. This is evident in his renovation of a 1940s-era estate, where he seamlessly added a new wing to balance the previously asymmetrical façade. The addition provides new guest suites, a sunroom featuring elliptical fanlights, and an oak-paneled drawing room centered on a George III–style marble mantel. The central block and east wing of the existing home were extensively renovated, stripping away the home's antiquated infrastructure and tired finishes, and bringing the home back to its original character.

House 10,000 ft² (929 m²)   Site 12 acres (4.85 ha)   Completion 2004

Interior designer Isabelle Vanneck (Davenport North LLC)   Lighting designer Gary Novasel (Patdo Lighting)

Landscape architect Charles J. Stick (Charles J. Stick Inc.)

Photography Nicholas Rotondi Photography; Stefen Turner Aerial Photography; Woodruff/Brown Architectural Photography; Charles Hilton Architects

Previous pages Boxwood hedges frame the view into the spacious yet comfortably scaled entry courtyard. The classically proportioned and detailed main body is flanked with two symmetrical wings that embrace guests and lead them in through the central portico. A custom brick blend was used on the new west wing addition (on right) to match the original brick and along with a variegated, semi-weathering Vermont slate blend around the house to complement the brick and mortar below.

Opposite An aerial view of the house's rear façade shows the architect's willingness to break from the strict symmetry of the front façade. While still employing classical proportions and composition, the south façade employs a variety of compositional elements in a balanced, asymmetrical composition. Also noteworthy is the careful balance and integration between the architecture and landscape design elements.

Above A view from the pool house looking across the pool terrace towards the south façade of the house. A series of classical windows, bays, dormers, and cupolas adorn the façade.

Following pages The two-story entry hall is simultaneously expansive and intimate with exquisite details throughout. The sweeping staircase and trompe l'oeil Adams ceiling and wall panels float gracefully over a radiating herringbone oak-and-walnut floor.

Above The east elevation of the new lattice sunroom features a trompe l'oeil lattice niche framing an antique limestone fountain beneath a Venetian plaster ceiling. Opposite The south and west elevations are framed with meticulously detailed lattice pilasters framing interior and exterior doors as well as custom commissioned artwork titles *Spring* and *Summer* by artist Robert Kushner.

Left The Great Room is housed in the new west wing of the residence. Classical oak paneling surrounds the custom reproduction George III Chesney's mantle and is capped by a dramatic coved plaster ceiling. Above A process sketch of the decorative frieze panel of the Georgian III mantel.

Following pages (left and middle) The elliptical staircase flows gracefully down from the second-floor bedrooms to the guest sitting room below. The walls are finished with a candy-apple green Venetian plaster. (right) View of the toile-themed guest suite overlooking the front entry court.

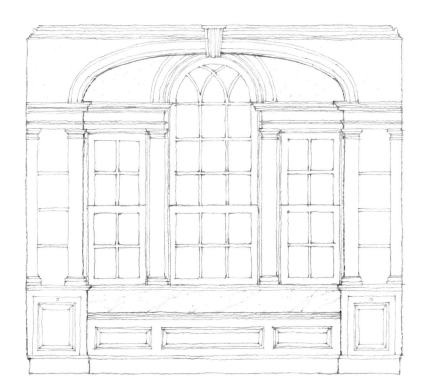

Left The first-floor guest suite opens out onto its own private terrace.
Above (Image and Sketch) The master bathtub niche enjoys expansive
views through its Palladian window to the gardens below.

Sleepy Cat Farm

Greenwich, Connecticut

The jewel in the crown of a 12-acre estate, and the crowning achievement of a 22-year relationship between client and architect, this French Norman farmhouse takes its inspiration from a trip Hilton made to Versailles. He translated the look and feel of the Norman-style, half-timber, thatch-roofed houses of the Queen's Hamlet, built for Marie Antoinette, to Greenwich. Here, he imagined a storybook French retreat with a steeply pitched slate roof and dormers, walls of heavy stonework, and half-timbering mixed with randomly laid terra-cotta Roman brick tiles. Hilton deploys European styles such as these when a project suggests a romantic aesthetic and relatively loose composition. Unlike Georgian estates, these European looks are less about rigor and formality, and more about the mood and feel of a place. They evoke not just the allure of a far-off destination, but the lifestyle enjoyed by those who live there. In the case of this home, the owners of which are avid gardeners and cooks who set out to turn their property into an organic farm, the Norman farmhouse style perfectly matched the substance of the program. Connection to the land emerged as a visual theme: A stone base anchors the home to the ground, and rustic or roughly hewn materials, used both inside and out, evoke the natural world.

House 6750 ft² (627 m²)   **Site** 12 acres (5 ha)   **Completion** 2013
Interior designer Isabelle Vanneck (Davenport North LLC)   **Lighting designer** Gary Novasel (Patdo Lighting)
Landscape architect Charles J. Stick (Charles J. Stick, Inc.)
Photography Woodruff/Brown Architectural Photography; Robert Benson Photography; Nicholas Rotondi Photography

Previous pages Guests approach from a winding antique cobblestone driveway to the lower level parking court. The stone base, which anchors the house to its rolling site, gives way to an antique timber post-and-beam frame with Roman brick infill. Opposite (top left) The south façade terrace sits nestled into the expansive classical gardens, which surround the house. (top right) View of the sun-drenched western façade. The upper façade is composed of an antique timber post-and-beam frame infilled with custom-made Ludowici Roman bricks. Each bay was set in a unique pattern to simulate the centuries old Norman architecture on which the home was based. (bottom) The home's main entry door is located on the south elevation and is surrounded by a carved classically inspired door surround. Above A view toward the garden façade and its tall timber bay, which is reminiscent of Lutyens's Deanery Garden.

Above Drawing study of the entry doorway. Right Wide oak doors welcome guests into the entry foyer, which is composed of Camargue limestone, rustic French-style plaster, and antique timbers on the walls and ceiling.

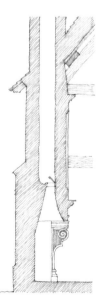

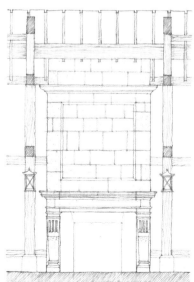

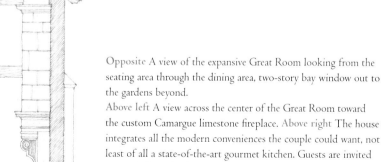

Opposite A view of the expansive Great Room looking from the seating area through the dining area, two-story bay window out to the gardens beyond.
Above left A view across the center of the Great Room toward the custom Camargue limestone fireplace. Above right The house integrates all the modern conveniences the couple could want, not least of all a state-of-the-art gourmet kitchen. Guests are invited to watch from the Great Room as gourmet food from the on-site organic farm is prepared in this rustic kitchen. Left Drawing study of the custom Carmague limestone fireplace.

Above The master bathroom wall, with a built-in vanity console, sits on a Thassos-marble mosaic floor.
Opposite A view of the expansive master bedroom located in the stone tower.
Following pages (left) A view of the master bedroom tower study. The tall sloped ceiling features
scenic elements from and around the property's extensive gardens. (right) The spiral stair corkscrews up
through the master bedroom's Venetian-plaster coved ceiling to the private study above.

Right The basement of the stone tower contains the timber framed wine cellar.

Waterfront Shingle Residence

Riverside, Connecticut

No aesthetic is more closely associated with classic coastal American retreats than the Shingle Style. Especially in the Northeast, rambling, wooden-shake-covered homes have dotted the seafront since the end of the 19th century, capturing the imaginations of ocean lovers for generations. Hilton has mastered the careful calculus required to maximize a home's water views and natural light. In Greenwich, his seaside homes stretch out along the shore, long and loose, to better take advantage of their broad vistas and southern exposure over Long Island Sound. A certain casual elegance defines the six-bedroom home here. Relatively closed and reserved on its front façade, the rear of the house, facing the water, opens up with large expanses of windows and glass doors, plus porches and pergolas that serve as alfresco rooms. Organic elements, curving shapes, and playful gestures soften the symmetry and angles of the façades and rooflines. Inside, formal herringbone floors, deeply carved balustrades, and layers of molding mix with more fanciful surprises—a breakfast room whose ceiling evokes the underside of a boat's deck, a study whose curve of windows suggests a ship's prow. Bead board appears on walls and ceilings throughout, as it would have in seaside cottages of an earlier era.

House 10,200 ft² (948 m²) **Site** 2 acres (0.8 ha) **Completion** 2013

Interior designer Amy Andrews (Hilton Interiors) **Lighting designer** Gary Novasel (Patdo Lighting) **Landscape architect** Bill Rutherford (Rutherford Associates, P.C.) **Photography** Woodruff/Brown Architectural Photography; Robert Benson Photography; Stefen Turner Aerial Photography; Nicholas Rotondi Photography

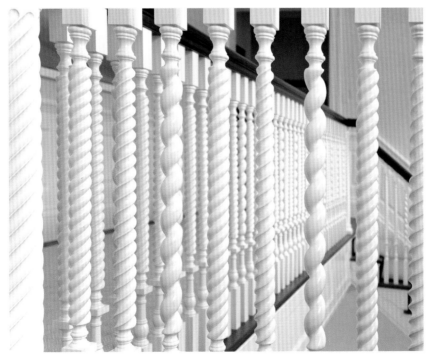

Previous pages The front façade of the residence has large sweeping roofs and a rustic stone base that stretches across the picturesque site. These pages A large entry foyer with its beamed ceiling, paneled walls, playful staircase and antiqued herringbone floor welcomes guests to the waterside retreat.

Opposite The bleached wood finish of the kitchen cabinets, soft hues of green and beige colors seen in the ceiling and countertops, and the distressed wood floors connect this kitchen with the rustic waterfront setting beyond.

Left and above A large, arched opening frames the view of the dining room from the living room.

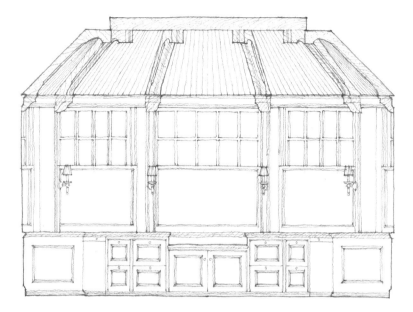

These pages The semi-circular master study enjoys commanding
180-degree views of Manhattan to Long Island across Long Island Sound.

Left The semi-circular round sitting porch enjoys panoramic views of Long Island Sound. Above Detail of the waterside pergola toward the master balcony. Following pages The residence's rear façade as seen from across the pool terrace.

FRANCK & LOHSEN ARCHITECTS

Franck & Lohsen's approach to traditional architecture is to create unique, livable, and timeless spaces. The firm's work is quite varied and ranges from urban homes to farmhouses and beach retreats. Clients are forward-thinking and want to build in a timeless manner that will ensure the longevity of their investment. Partners Michael Franck and Art Lohsen enjoy the opportunity to work with some of the best interior designers who infuse the built works with an energy, a personality and a calm commensurate with the unique taste of each client.

Franck & Lohsen has been recognized by the most important organization that represents the ongoing renaissance of traditional and classical architecture. The Institute of Classical Architecture and Art awarded its prestigious Arthur Ross Award for Architecture to Franck & Lohsen. Despite unparalleled credentials in classical architecture, the word 'classical' is not the first adjective that the partners use to describe their work. "Timeless is a much better word," says Michael Franck. "The most important aspect of great classical architecture is that it is just as beautiful, relevant, and accessible now as when it was first conceived."

After years of study, travel, apprenticing with noted classical architects, and working with many clients around the world, Franck & Lohsen has developed an expertise that, while classically based, often transcends strict delineations of style and precedent. With offices in Washington, D.C. and Savannah, Georgia, Franck & Lohsen's style has a definite Southern lilt at times, a reflection of Michael Franck's Southern roots. First and foremost, with each project is the notion that the firm's work should look like it has 'always been there'.

"Truly great architecture is the result of the collaboration between the architect, the client, and the builder," explains Art Lohsen. "The reason that Michael and I are successful is that we work so well as a team. We do much better work together, and it is much more fun." This collaborative approach has enabled the firm to design homes that are firmly grounded in their region and site, but are also fresh and contemporary. Each project is elegant, beautiful, and mature, while at the same time meeting the needs and tastes of a new generation of younger clients.

"American homes are all about practicality and comfort. Our clients want an interesting and innovative home that reflects their personality, while at the same time being a good neighbor," says Franck. "And by getting to know each of our clients, we are able to deliver that. In the end, we have both a beautiful, timeless new home and a wonderful new friendship."

"True beauty is timeless, which is why we strive for true timelessness in our work."

A Farmhouse

Princeton, New Jersey

Serving as a private residence, this new farmhouse anchors a 100-acre (40.5-hectare) property that features an organic farm, a farmer's market and a therapeutic riding facility. The first building on this new farm was the family home, which was designed in keeping with the local vernacular architecture, including fieldstone, brick, and clapboard. Timeless materials, such as hand-crimped copper and Vermont slate are in harmony with the stone and brick. Mahogany windows with operable shutters add a quality and authenticity to the house. True leaded glass is used on the fanlight and the side lights of the front door. By designing the new house with a large central mass with several flanking wings or "additions," this house was built to look like it grew over time. Perched on a knoll at the center of the property and in line with an existing hedgerow, the farmhouse commands a central position, joining together the variety of functions that coexist on the farm while also meeting the needs of a large family. A walled vegetable garden helps anchor the house to the property and blends seamlessly into the landscape. Other buildings on the property include a free-standing farm office built with the same fieldstone as the main body of the house. Nestled into the landscape and located at a fork in a newly created drive this new building denotes the precinct of the family area and the farm area.

House 7100 ft² (660 m²)   Site 100 acres (40.5 ha)   Completion 2013

Interiors Spurgeon Lewis   **Landscape architect** Jay Graham

Photography Gordon Beall

Left Timeless materials are used on both the exterior and the interior of the house with the kitchen and family dining areas using wood flooring and historically salvaged interior paneling giving the feeling that this new kitchen has been around for a long time. Above The interior of the house has areas that are more formal, namely in the entry hall and the library, while the rest of the house gracefully accommodates the rambunctious nature of the growing family.

An Estate on the Water

Glen Echo, Maryland

There are very few sites near Washington, D.C. that combine dramatic natural views with a short drive to downtown. Thought to be unbuildable, this steeply sloped site was constrained by National Park Land on one side and a neighboring house on the other. With such a unique site at the bend of the Potomac River, Franck & Lohsen designed a house that took full advantage of these remarkable views by developing a "butterfly plan" house with wings that reached out at angles into the site. Stylistically, the exterior recalls the historic country houses of Sir Edwin Lutyens who used brick, clay-tile roofing, imposing chimneys and deviated from a staid architecture.

This dynamic house features a formal front façade with an undulating façade both in plan and in elevation to reflect the movement of the river beyond. The wings on each side of the rear of the house enclose a two-story terrace overlooking a large new pool as well as the great river below. "By angling the wings, we were able to perfectly frame the views up and down the Potomac River, while shielding the rear terrace from the neighbors," explains Art Lohsen. "The way this home opens out into the landscape and takes full advantage of such a unique site is really quite special," says Michael Franck.

House 14,000 ft² (1,300 m²) **Site** 2 acres (0.8 ha) **Completion** 2013

Interior designer Darryl Carter **Consulting architect** Bruce Hayes **Landscape architect** Caroline Ervin

Hardscaping design Franck & Lohsen Architects **Photography** Gordon Beall

Opposite A split winding staircase embraces the front entry to the house and echoes the flow of the Potomac River beyond. Hand-hewn herringbone wood floor adds texture and a depth of color to the formal rooms of the house. Above left A unique circular-shaped breakfast room with a domed ceiling offers a panoramic view of the Potomac River and brings light into the room at all times of the day from sunrise to sunset. Above right A family staircase is nestled into the hallway and is of a similar quality to the main staircase. Historic and antique lighting throughout the house adds a timeless look and feel.

71

Right A generous family kitchen combines beauty and practicality. A large island plays host to bar style seating, cabinets below for storage of large pots and pans, and does double duty as a buffet table when the family entertains. The range wall is bracketed by large pantry cabinets, which are both convenient and elegant. Wall cabinets that bracket the generous window also boast cabinets that extend to the counter which hide all the small appliances and gadgets keeping the overall look clean and organized. A window seat provides a respite as well as storage.

Above A sumptuous master bathroom for the lady of the house combines beauty and practicality. The dressing room and closet is off to the left while a vanity at the windows provides natural lighting. The large soaking tub is surrounded by marble and antiqued mirrors and is bracketed by a shower on one side and the water closet on the other side. A soft band of pink marble in the floor separates a field of herringbone tile from the border of larger pieces of marble. A custom sink vanity with many drawers helps keep this room organized and elegant.

Opposite Her office is located on one of the wings of the butterfly plan and provides views out three directions, providing light throughout the day. The room has a square shape offering a calm and intimate scale with highly detailed moldings, custom cabinetry and an antique marble mantelpiece. An intimate desk area is in the bay window.

Opposite The rear of the house faces a bend in the Potomac River. The unique butterfly plan, which has a wing on each side, embraces the river and provides containment and privacy for the family. The house boasts a Ludowici tile roof, ornately detailed cornices and finely executed brickwork. Rooms on the main level all open on to a bluestone terrace for spectacular view of the river. This terrace overlooks the pool below but doesn't allow for the pool always to be front and center.

Above Underneath the bluestone terrace is a long linear loggia at the pool level and boasts a series of "handkerchief" vaults that create a unique ceiling and a dramatic, yet intimate, series of rooms. This end of the loggia has a fireplace and a generous seating area. The other end of the loggia has a large grilling area and a large family table. (Gas fixture by Bevolo of New Orleans.)

A Classic Colonial Revival

Washington, D.C.

Located on one of the most well-known residential streets in Washington, this historic stone house had never met its potential and had been the victim to ill-advised additions and curious alterations over the last few decades. Franck & Lohsen was asked not only to return the house to its original grandeur, but also to expand it to meet the needs of an active family.

The first phase of the project was to gut the interior and restore a center hall to the house. A new grand stair was designed to connect not only to the bedrooms above, but also to a new planned kitchen addition. By locating this stair off the main axis of the house, the rooms intended for entertaining could be larger and more elegantly connected to each other and to the beautiful gardens. This center hall brings visitors through to an expanded rear terrace with a commanding view over the existing pool and tennis court. Connections among the terraced garden levels were improved and a large sun room was added to overlook the gardens.

On the front façade, a new entry portico and three new dormer windows complete the transformation of this house from an ugly duckling into a beautiful and grand home.

House 12,000 ft² (1115 m²) **Site** 1 acre (0.4 ha) **Completion** 2015 (Phase I)

Interior designer Lauren Liess **Landscape architect** Scott Brinitzer

Photography Helen Norman

Previous pages (left) Having been victim to numerous timid renovations this house was in bad need of straightening out the bones. The new entry hall was created when the entire interior of the house was gutted. It serves as the principal organizing room on the main level. Bold new classical millwork, designed to house a series of four antique gouache paintings, anchors the room. A wall of antiqued mirrors extends the view of the new stair hall, while antique marble floors provide a timeless look and feel. (right) A bold new staircase set apart from the principle rooms serves as the family access to the upper levels. Light floods in from the new dormers that were added to the front of the house. A dynamic light fixture and custom metal railing add a modern touch to this newly renovated house. Opposite A two-story addition was placed on the side of the house to house this sun room and a master bathroom above. The was designed to look as though an older porch was enclosed in a previous era to give a feeling of timelessness. New honed limestone floors work beautifully with the original stone wall of the main house. Above This new library looks like it's always been there. The custom mahogany book cases with Doric pilasters frame a new bolection mantelpiece. A new custom plaster ceiling adds detail in an often-overlooked area of a room.

Opposite The new living room joined what was originally two rooms. A bay window was added and offers great views into the large backyard and floods the living room with light. Bold pilasters anchor the bay window and a robust cornice ties the room together and contrasts nicely with the dedicated plaster detail on the ceiling. Above left Her dressing room is light-filled and finely detailed with custom cabinetry for hanging, shelves, shoes, etc. Ebony-stained floors contrast with crisp white cabinetry and a wallpapered ceiling. A unique mid-century modern chandelier completes the look. Above right The new master bathroom follows suit with the sun room below by making the room appear as though it was a porch that was closed in over time. A bold marble floor in a chevron pattern provides a modern vibe, which contrasts nicely with the Doric columns. A custom vanity and mirror on each side of the room gives him and her their own areas. A custom nickel-and-glass shower enclosure is a main feature in the room.

An English Cottage

Washington, D.C.

While serving as vice president, Richard Nixon and his wife Pat lived in this charming English country–style house in northwest Washington, D.C. As with many houses of that period, there was a strong separation of public and service spaces, with an isolated kitchen and separate rooms and stairs for staff.

When a young family purchased this house, there was a desire to renovate, not only to open the house up to be less formal but also to add additional space. By combining rooms and opening the plan, Franck & Lohsen was able to accommodate all of the client's needs without the need for an addition. A small bar area was converted to an office, and an enclosed porch became a small study, and a new master bathroom and closets took over what had been a spare bedroom. A large new bay window was installed to take advantage of views across the rear yard to the adjacent park land. The finished project is a wonderful blend of grown-up formality and funky finishes.

On the front, the house is nicely nestled into the mature landscape. The rear yard had a very steep slope overlooking national parkland. Working with the landscape architect, Franck & Lohsen was able to create a series of terraces, a pool and a large lawn that serves double duty as a temporary indoor hockey rink, which is erected during the winter months.

House 9500 ft² (883 m²)   **Site** 1 acre (0.4 ha) **Completion** 2010

Interior designer Maria Crosby Pollard   **Landscape architect** Jamie Walsh

Photography Gordon Beall

Previous pages This charming English cottage–style house is made from fieldstone, limestone accents and terra-cotta roof tiles. The mature look and feel contrasts nicely with the youthful and light-filled interiors. Above The living room as seen through the Gothic-styled archway from the entry hall. All the wood in the ceiling had to be straightened, leveled and was then stripped to reveal the original cerused finish. Right New custom doors and windows were made to match the cerused oak finish prevalent throughout the house. The youthful yet timeless decoration makes for a perfect complement to this historic house.

Following pages (left) The main staircase was renovated and restored to its original look and feel. Elements that were missing, such as the post, were pulled from historic documents and replicated. Originally there was a wall shielding the kitchen and service areas of the house from the public rooms. The removal of such walls opened up the house as seen in the view beyond to the new kitchen. (right) Previously the formal dining room, this family room was opened up with a new Gothic-style opening with pocket doors to what was originally the butler's pantry, which was repurposed to be a more family friendly dining area. A new paneled wainscot adds detail to the room, which is enhanced by a fun wallpaper ceiling and comfortable yet stylish furniture.

Left The new family kitchen was originally a service kitchen, a serving pantry, and a small staff dining area. These rooms were all eliminated and the space reconfigured to create a modern kitchen with ample storage and lots of light. A classic cork floor adds softness and durability. Above The family dining features a custom banquette and a striped pattern in the cork flooring.

An Urban House

Washington, D.C.

This house, built in the late 1960s, is at heart a five-part Palladian villa. Unfortunately, it was designed at a time when that was not fashionable, and the original architect did his best on the exterior to make it look "of its time." When Franck & Lohsen was asked to renovate the house for a young family, it was clearly in need of significant work.

The starting point was to bring the house back to its classically inspired roots. The façades were adjusted to provide direct access to the garden at the rear, and the front balcony was converted to a more delicate feature. On the exterior, a new bluestone terrace was created to transition from the rear of the home to a new formal rear lawn. What had been a forgotten rear yard became the new center of family activity.

In order to provide handicap access from a lower level guest suite to the rest of the house, a new elevator was added. The oversized kitchen was re-organized and enhanced with new custom cabinetry and appliances. The renovated home occupies its corner lot with a quiet and effortless grace. Art Lohsen reflects "Some of the neighbors don't believe it is the same house!"

House 9850 ft² (915 m²)   **Site** 0.5 acre (0.2 ha)   **Completion** 2010

Interior designer Darryl Carter   **Landscape architect** Jamie Walsh

Photography Gordon Beall

Right Almost all interior rooms were significantly altered, most notably the entry hall where a new sweeping circular staircase replaced an uninspired and not very functional one. A new large landing helps to break up the long entry hall into two more appropriately scaled spaces. Following pages (left) View into the living room with the dining room beyond. A repurposing of the rooms helped to create a better flow and to maximize the uses of the spaces. The previous dining room is now used as a family room. (right) This former dining room serves as the nexus of activity for the family and is close to the kitchen and the outdoor terrace. A custom bookcase humanizes the scale of the room and adds a level of detail that appears original to the house. The decoration adds a layered look that enhances the timeless nature of this newly renovated house.

A Seaside Retreat

Rehoboth Beach, Delaware

Inspired by the Creole Style architecture of Louisiana that the client had grown to love as a child, this new beach house was designed as a weekend retreat for a large family. In keeping with the Creole vernacular and to offer the best views of the surrounding marsh, the primary floor is located on the second level.

Those rooms most used by the family face the rear of the house, which opens to a large screened porch with an outdoor kitchen and dining area. A swimming pool and terrace area is raised above grade to catch the view and breezes, but remains beneath the sight lines from the main living rooms above.

The upper floors have six bedrooms and a large bunk room centered around a family hallway. At ground level are a guest suite and play room as well as the family entry and covered parking on a loop drive beneath the screened porch above.

House 5000 ft² (465 m²) **Site** 0.5 acre (0.2 ha) **Completion** 2016

Interior designer Maria Crosby Pollard **Hardscape design** Franck & Lohsen Architects

Photography Gordon Beall

Above The entry hall pairs the unique screen door with a traditional fan light and side lights. The youthful decoration of the house also takes full advantage of the seaside location, while painted floors throughout reduces the formality of the house.

Opposite The large open family room and kitchen serves as the heart of the home and features wood paneled ceilings and robust millwork in contrast to the more contemporary kitchen beyond.

Following pages (left) The master bathroom is unique in the use of a random pattern of hexagonal concrete pavers in a range of grays and black colors. The vertical siding on the walls makes for more of a coastal look and feel. (right) The lower level of the house has two guest suites, including this well-loved play room/bunk room. Waterworks brick tiles keep the floors bright, fresh and easy to clean from sandy feet coming in from the beach.

HAMADY ARCHITECTS

Architecture is the marriage between the collective art and craft of building and the nature of the landscape in which it resides. The architect's role is to fully understand each particular condition prior to altering the natural landscape and reshape it into a new cultural context. Each building becomes the enduring and meaningful representation of those understandings, the universal design principles applied and the spiritual, intellectual, emotional, and physical energies vested into it. Being comprehensive and purposefully meaningful, Architecture requires collaboration with sister subjects. From the center where the patron stands, the architect and the master builder rely on surrounding circles, each contributing to the final results. Architecture is ultimately a revealing measure of the cultural development of a civilized society.

Established in 1997 by Kahlil Hamady, the design firm is founded on first and foremost, the profound understanding of the natural and cultural landscapes of each project. The designs of the firm are rooted in a deep respect for nature and in each project's particular cultural context. Its efforts are based on historical and time-tested principles and patterns that inform and guide the design process. The firm relies on traditional methods of design and illustration through hand drawings and paintings and on the traditional arts and crafts of building. Each project traditionally begins with the development of a comprehensive master plan that is informed by the inextricable relationship between architecture, landscape design and interior decoration and is carried through the design of the finest details.

The firm's efforts have been recognized by the Institute of Classical Architecture and Art. The firm has been the recipient of four Stanford White Awards: in 2013 (for two projects), 2014 and 2016, one John Russell Pope Award in 2015, a Charles Bulfinch Award in 2016, and a 2015 National Palladio Award.

The key design professionals associated with the firm are Kahlil Hamady, Peter Lorenzoni, Mark Jackson and Leslie-jon Vickory.

"As a container of individual and collective memory, Architecture is a meaningful and enduring representation of a civilized society. Its protection represents the moral thread that preserves the records and identity of a culture."

Cricket Hill

Greenwich, Connecticut

Beautifully sited toward an expansive vista overlooking a lake, the original Georgian country house was designed in 1930 by architect and conservationist, Erard A. Mattiessen.

In 2005, the current homeowners engaged the firm to renovate and carefully expand on the existing house with new wings while enhancing the original architectural and landscape composition of the property. With close attention to the classical principles that guided the original design and great awareness to the essential relationships between the landscape and the architectural spaces, organizing axes were extended vertically and horizontally from the central hall through the primary spaces of the house and into the landscape beyond.

By preserving the modest scale of the original house, the architecture of the additions and renovations maintained a restrained and measured articulation of space. The proportions of the volumes and the exterior and interior surfaces were refined with disciplined attention to precision and detail.

House 10,000 ft² (929 m²) **Site** 11 acres (4.5 ha) **Completion** 2005

Interior designer Bunny Williams, Bunny Williams Interior Design **Landscape architect** Wertimer and Associates

Craftspeople Gaston and Wyatt; CJS **Photography** Robert Llewellyn

Previous pages (top left) Detailed view of entablature of the new portico.
(bottom left) Detail of new window and masonry at west façade.
(right) View of new forecourt and recomposed east façade. Above The
view of the new central hall stairway from the dining room. Left View of
the new three-level stairway culminating with a designed trompe l'oeuil of a
domed ceiling.

Clockwise from opposite top left Detailed view of new vaulted passage at vestibule to lakeside terrace; Axial view from new library and gallery through renovated living room, central stair hall and study; Detail at library of a hand-carved wood capital showing an acorn as a symbol of some of the indigenous landscape that the house originally replaced; Drawing of the Ionic Order composition for the library; View of living room interior millwork and paneling; View of new interior millwork and paneling in living room showing marble fireplace mantel selected by interior designer, Bunny Williams.

Previous pages View of west façade showing redesign and proportions of central
composition as well as the north and south wing additions.
Above Trellis detail at pool terrace. **Opposite** View of trellised kitchen terrace.
Following pages View of the south wing addition. The sequential arrangement
of the outdoor and indoor spaces was carefully examined starting with the entry
to the property, through the house and out again into the larger landscape.

A Neo-colonial House

Greenwich, Connecticut

Located in an intimate neighborhood surrounding a central park, the original Neo-colonial country house was constructed in 1920. In 2014, the current homeowners engaged the firm to renovate the existing residence and carefully expand it with a new wing while enhancing the original architectural and landscape composition of the property. With close attention to the classical principles that guided the original design and great awareness of the essential relationships between the landscape and the architectural spaces, the sequential arrangement of the outdoor and indoor spaces was carefully examined starting with the entry to the property, the driveway, the first impression of the house, the arrival to the forecourt, the entry though the front porch, the house and out into the larger landscape. The axii are used as tools for weaving the compositional relationships between internal and external spaces, the house and the gardens, and the organization of the interior spaces bring more utility to the interior and exterior spaces according to classical principles of design. There is a reinforcement of a sense of permanence through the introduction of carved elements with materials that gave a sense of warmth and timelessness while weaving the history of the family with the house.

House 3500 ft² (325 m²)   **Site** 4 acres (1.62 ha)   **Completion** 2014

Interior designer Suzanne Kasler   **Landscape designer** Kathryn Herman, Doyle Herman Design Associates

Craftspeople Gaston and Wyatt; Nantz Hardware; La Cornue; Rangecraft   **Photography** Robert Llewellyn

Left View from park of the layered outdoor spaces and the renovated south façade. Top View of entrance to new addition through enclosed west garden. Bottom View of new south portico. Following page, clockwise from top left The west garden, viewed from dining room terrace; The north family terrace viewed from the rear garden; View of new trellis at the east terrace.

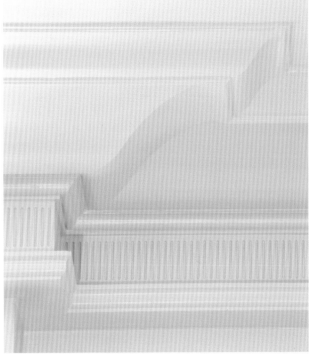

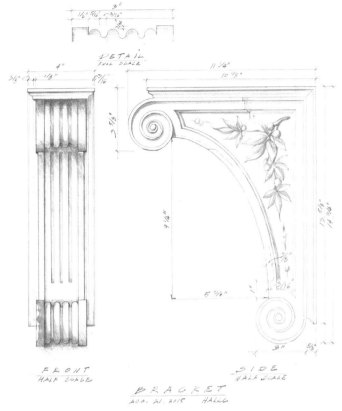

Previous page (left) Interior axial and framed view from entrance foyer and stairhall through dining room, the trellised terrace and enclosed garden. (top right) Detail at cornice at central stair hall. (bottom right) View of extended stair from cellar to third floor. Opposite Axial view from new kitchen through breakfast room, family room, trellised terrace to future formal garden. The calibration of the interior millwork creates a sense of height with the use of attenuated and elongated details. Top left Details of hand-carved wood brackets at bar representing the buckeye tree. Above Design drawing of bracket at new bar. Left Detail of hand-carved wood panel at bar fireplace symbolizing the family heritage.

Mill Mountain Farm

Albemarle County, Virginia

Bordering mountains and hills give the property a private and sheltered character to the heart of the farm. At its center, a circular knoll stands surrounded by a stone wall around which hills and mountains radiate beyond. Close to the center of the knoll, a Sycamore tree is firmly planted. The house was sited at the northern edge of the central fields, at the boundary between the fields and the forest. The approach to the site follows a long drive starting at an entry over a creek and a gentle and curving ascent through woodlands with a final approach to the east side of the house. The lines of the landscape defined by the topography and the curving road extend into the architectural axis defining the spine of the house. With its back retaining a gentle slope, the house radiates toward the southern views, offering the house and its rooms the capture of the sun- and moonlights in addition to the pleasant breezes through the fields. The composition was fundamentally sculptural in its intent, with respect to natural forms and the traditional order of architectural procession through public and private spaces.

House 6000 ft² (557 m²)   **Site** 600 acre (243 ha)   **Completion** 2010

Interior designers Kahlil Hamady; Leslie-jon Vickory   **Interior furnishing consultant** Marquis & Francois

Photography Robert Llewellyn

Previous pages View of the house sited at the bottom of a south-facing slope where the mountain forest and the opened fields begin to meet. Above and right Views of the eastern approach to the house through the forest. The bending of the spine of the composition and the articulation of the forms and details of the house evoke the specific and general character of a Virginia landscape highlighting the relationship between the house and its landscape. Following pages (left) View of the entrance porch echoing the surrounding landscape forms. (right) View of the master bedroom pavilion.

Opposite (clockwise from top left) View of the south-facing living room porch; Detailed view of the living room porch; View of the curving family room and master bedroom facing the northern forested hill; View through a window of the living room Venetian draperies and lights.
Above View of the Northern side of the house echoing the form of the hill.
Following pages (left) View of the south-facing living room wing. The most public space, the living room and its porch projected the furthest toward the southern views while the dining receded into the woodland side and the family room straddled both. (right) View of the designed interiors and furnishings of the living room.

Above Detail of designed fireplace mantel and terra-cotta tiles at master
bedroom. Opposite Drawings of the dining room interiors and furnishings.
The design intent and results represent an adaptation of classical principles
to their particular cultural and natural environments with the purpose of
creating a contextual and architectural intervention.

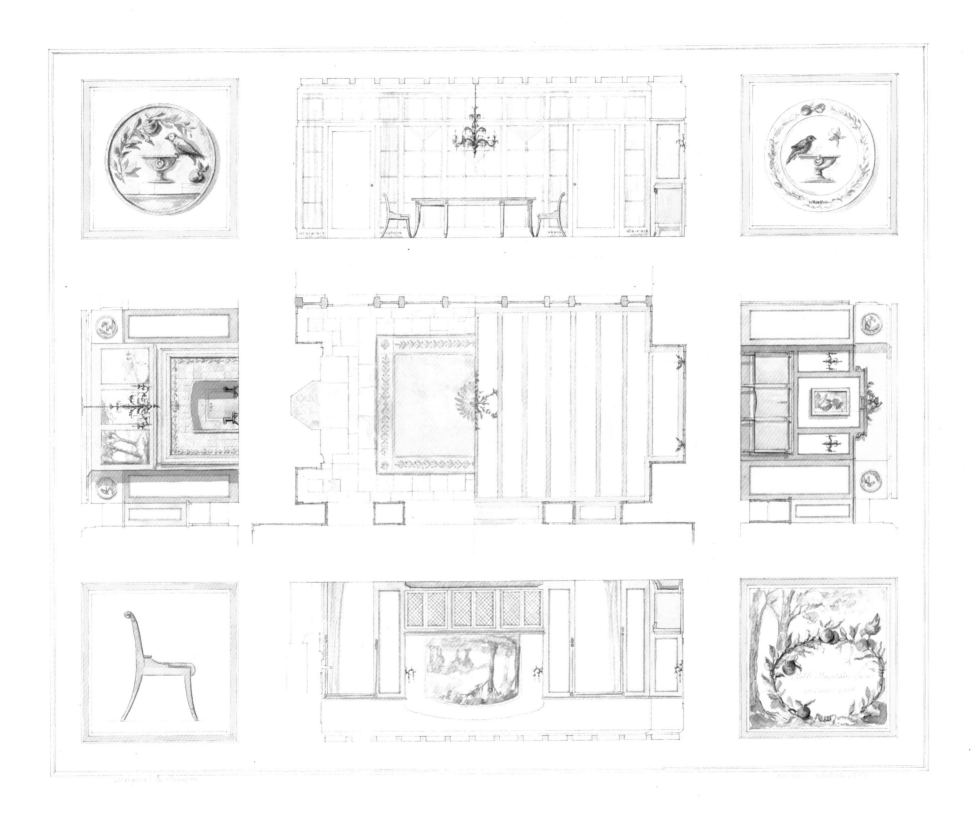

A Mountain Home

White Sulphur Springs, West Virginia

The site is located at the very tip of a mountain ridge, its land forming a semi-conical shape with steep hills on three sides. The westerly approach from a private road straddling the ridge brings the visitor to the end of the mountain, opening up to sweeping northern, easterly and southern vistas of valleys, fields and mountains. While the site offers dramatic and spectacular views, its topography and access presented challenges to the design for a large home with a vehicular forecourt, outdoor terraces and a garage.

In order to maintain harmonious relationships with the site and the surrounding landscape, the design included carving the crest of the hill, embedding the house into it, crafting architectural forms that evoke the shapes of the hills and finally crowning the land with a humanly scaled and proportioned intervention. The procession allows a gentle drive down toward the south of the property, leading into a porte-cochere and a garage that retains the front western landmass of the property. Despite its topographical challenge, the house ultimately offers its owners a home that harmoniously weaves their cultural identity with the natural landscape.

House 6000 ft² (557 m²) **Site** 15 acres (6 ha) **Completion** 2010

Interior designer Carolyn Tucks, Someday Interiors **Contractor** Rob Vass, Sterling Construction

Photography Robert Llewellyn

Previous pages View of the entry drive through the porte cochere. Opposite View of the northeast façade and terrace garden through the trellised walk from the garage. Top View of the northeast façade. Left View of the northeast garden from the secondary entrance. Above Detail of the roof cornice.

Above Partial watercolor drawing of the southwestern façade. In addition to the evocation of natural forms, the house harbors architectural elements that are culturally meaningful to the owners (i.e. the arched brackets stirring imagery of train stations, familiar to the legacies of the owners' family). Opposite View of the living room porch from the forecourt.

Following pages (left) View through the round window at foyer. (right) The most public space, the living room, was located in the center of the composition, bridging on a north-south axis a lawn terrace to the north overlooking a valley and a projecting stone fireplaced porch to the south that highlighted the relationship of the house with its surrounding landscape.

JOHN MILNER ARCHITECTS

The principals of John Milner Architects describe their firm as a collaborative team of design professionals that honors the continuum of architecture by creating new buildings inspired by classical American and European traditions, and also by preserving historic buildings, which connect them to a unique and diverse cultural heritage. John Milner established the firm on that premise in the era of the American Bicentennial Celebration. He was later joined by his partners Mary Werner DeNadai and Christopher Miller, and by colleagues Christina Carter, Justin Detwiler, Patrick McDonough, Scott O'Barr, Brad Roeder and Edward Wheeler. Together with the firm's design and technical studio members, they embrace the belief that understanding how challenges were met and resolved by clients, architects and artisans in the past empowers them to consider precedent in formulating contemporary design solutions. Since preservation and restoration have always been an integral part of their practice, they are well versed in the architectural fundamentals and details represented by a broad range of time periods and styles.

The principles of classicism are with the firm throughout its entire design process for a new house, beginning with the selection of the site and formulating a response to the particular environmental characteristics of that place. The site provides direction, often leading to a solution that will best interpret the clients' desires within a specific context. Creating a sense of discovery is an important component of the firm's design approach, so that the features of the house and its integration with the site are sequentially revealed. For projects involving the restoration and adaptation of historic buildings, respecting the intent of the original designers and preserving significant character-defining features are hallmarks of responsible stewardship. Celebrating the building crafts has long played a prominent role in the firm's work, because the craftsmen's contributions to a project are essential to realizing, enriching and giving personality to the final creation. When considering the effect of classical design on everyday life, one of the firm's clients offered a succinct observation, quoted below.

"The house has a definite order to it, which promotes a life of simplicity and organization. Each room seems to have its own particular purpose, evoking a sense of intimacy, privacy and solitude. It is almost like a collection of sanctuaries."

NEW COUNTRY HOUSE

Villanova, Pennsylvania

The designs of Sir Edwin Lutyens and his interpretations of classicism were also on the minds of both the client and architects who designed the house to capture those qualities while serving the needs of an active family. The exterior design features vernacular materials blended with traditional and more formal Georgian elements and detailing.

The interior features a first-floor enfilade connecting the formal and informal spaces, incorporating the main staircase, and providing a sense of transparency enhanced by abundant natural light from large windows in the flanking spaces. The more formal spaces include a foyer, living room, dining room and library, each with expansive views of the surrounding landscape. Close connections are created between the house and landscape, which features outdoor spaces for all seasons, including an orchid house, pool garden with a pavilion, rose gardens, extensive cutting gardens and outdoor terraces. The gardens transition from structured and formal to natural and wild, providing borrowed views of a rolling agrarian landscape.

House 8500 ft² (790 m²) **Site** 17 acres (6.9 ha) **Completion** 2006
Interior designer Gauthier-Stacy Inc. **Landscape architect** Jonathan Alderson Landscape Architects
Contractor Griffiths Construction, Inc. **Photography** Matt Wargo Architectural Photographer; Tom Crane Photography

On the books:

EDWIN LUTYENS
THE GREATER PERFECTION
Lesieur

Previous pages (left) The front entrance features a carved Indiana limestone door surround and leaded glass transom. The exterior light fixture is an antique English sconce. (right) The entry hall with its front doors ajar leads out with views to the entry court beyond. Opposite The library is shown with ornamental plaster ceiling and ebonized bookcases stretching from floor to ceiling.
Above The interior design contrasts fine quality traditional detailing with a more contemporary aesthetic to create a lively living environment. A stone and copper fireplace surround with raised limestone hearth adorns the family room, which is adjacent to the kitchen.

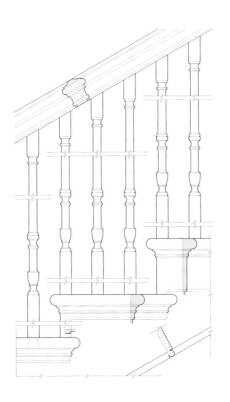

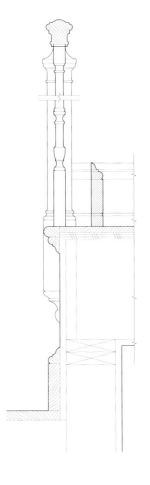

Opposite The formal dining room features a paneled fireplace and leads through to the living room and stair hall beyond. The high ceilings and relatively unadorned plaster walls comfortably accommodate the clients' varied art collections. Top left Detail of neoclassical mantel with hand-carved swags and brackets. Top right View through the enfilade looking from base of main stair through entry hall to library hall beyond. Above and right Details of stair components, including curtailed stair tread and custom-turned balusters.

SHINGLE STYLE RESIDENCE

Atlantic County, New Jersey

This new residence occupies a unique position on the New Jersey shore, with expansive sandy beaches on two sides and spectacular views to the north, east and south. In keeping with the traditional Shingle Style vernacular architecture of the mid-Atlantic coast, the architects created a home that takes advantage of the site's unique features, while also maintaining traditional Shingle Style details and proportions. The façade features two-toned cedar shingles, painted brackets and paneling and a Vermont slate roof. The plan is oriented with the second floor serving as the primary level to allow for better views of the ocean, with the first and third floors serving secondary spaces. The first floor contains a formal entry hall, and spaces for entertaining that open onto the main deck, outdoor kitchen and swimming pool.

Throughout the house, interior millwork is detailed in keeping with the Shingle Style and features beadboard patterned ceilings, full-height paneled walls and numerous built-in cabinets and benches.

House 5600 ft² (520 m²)   Site 9000 ft² (836 m²)   **Completion** 2016
Interior designer Eberlein Design Consultants Ltd.   **Landscape architect** Robinson Anderson Summers, Inc.
Contractor Cherokee Construction   **Photography** Tom Crane Photography

Previous pages Northeast elevation at dusk, showcasing how the second and first floors feature flared shingle façades that mimic traditional Shingle Style homes of the region. The third floor features commanding views of the ocean from a private deck. Opposite clockwise from top left Entry doors looking through northeast loggia; Ipe decking rises up and over the existing bulkhead and creates a bench that wraps two sides of the property for easy access to the beach, seen here across the northeast loggia with the ocean beyond; Entry hall looking towards front door and main stair; Main stair between first and second floors. Above Living room looking east. Exterior windows and doors are maximized to allow for sweeping views of the ocean beyond.

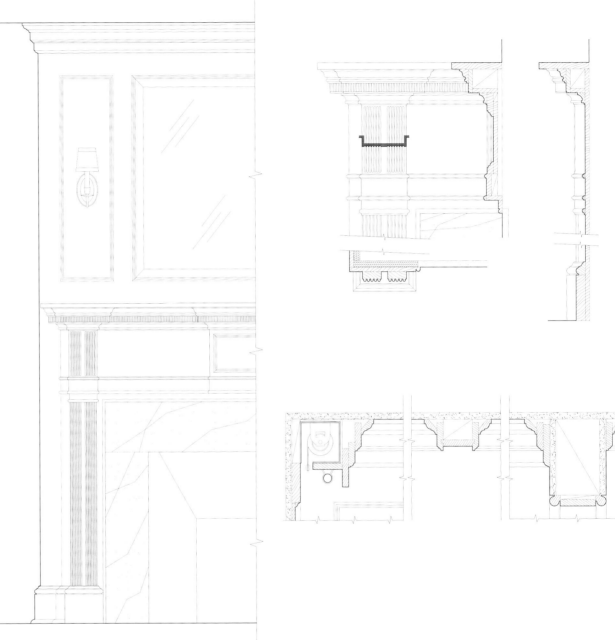

Left The second, or primary floor, features a formal living room, a dining room that connects to the open kitchen and an enclosed porch. This level is wrapped by an open balcony that overlooks the deck and pool below, with sweeping views of the ocean beyond. Above Custom-designed white-oak mantel details were inspired by mid-19th-century examples from the region.

GOTHIC REVIVAL CHAPEL

Philadelphia, Pennsylvania

Built between 1876 and 1880, this chapel in the Gothic Revival style was designed by architect James Peacock Sims, and expanded in 1892 according to the designs of architect Frank Furness. Set discretely in the context of mid-19th-century rowhouses in Philadelphia, the scale and rhythm of the façade complements its neighbors and presents a subtle surprise within the traditional streetscape. The guiding principle of the project was to preserve the building's distinctive exterior and interior architectural character while carefully introducing key elements in support of the transition to residential use, with expansive and private outdoor space in the heart of the city. The exterior façades with gothic window and door openings, patterned brickwork, decorative wood detailing, and dramatic slate roof were restored. A single-car garage was inserted and a small glass pavilion was added on the courtyard side to provide a connection to the garden and outdoor views from the entrance. Intimate areas were created for dining, sitting, music, and entertaining. The historic chapel's solemn grandeur endures in harmony with its new contemporary residential use.

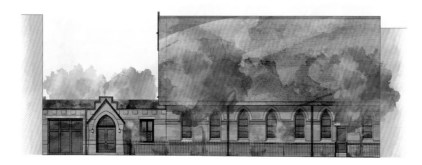

House 5300 ft² (492 m²)   **Site** 6600 ft² (613 m²)   **Completion** 2016

Contractor Cherokee Construction

Photography Tom Crane Photography

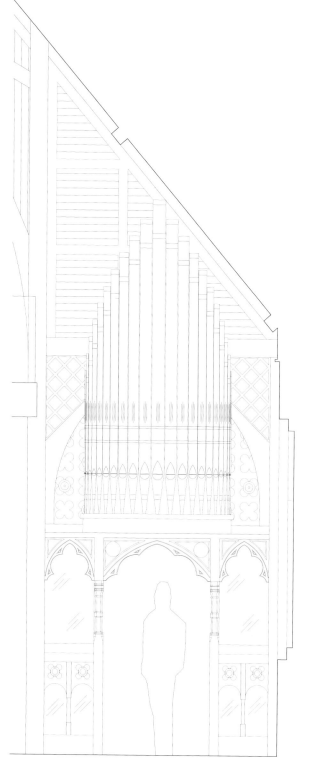

Opposite The nave (looking east), with its soaring trussed wood ceiling, painted brick walls, and leaded glass windows, naturally became the primary gathering space. Left Although the organ was removed, the two sets of painted organ pipes were carefully restored and re-installed flanking the balcony. Above Detail showing the reinstalled organ pipes.

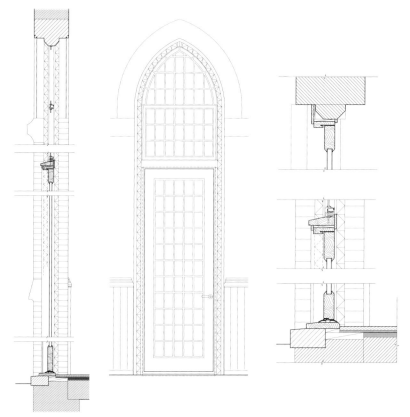

Top and right The chancel was transformed into a two-level library, partially screened from the nave on the lower level by the addition of a custom concrete-clad gas fireplace in the living area. Above An existing leaded glass window was modified and a wood and leaded glass door was inserted to provide direct access to the courtyard.

Top Secondary spaces such as the kitchen, with a breakfast area within a glass pavilion, bedrooms and related functions, all with views and access to the garden, were placed adjacent to the principal living space in the nave. Right Details of the glass pavilion include expansive window openings and integrated motorized shades concealed behind a wood cornice. Opposite Kitchen with original arched openings looking through to entry hall beyond.

AGINCOURT

Chester County, Pennsylvania

Agincourt is a new Tudor Style residence situated on one of the largest intact properties on Philadelphia's storied Main Line. The house was placed on a gently sloping portion of the site to take maximum advantage of southern, eastern and western vistas across the landscape. Unique spaces include a home theater; a recreation room with antique bar; a music room that resembles a jazz club; and an indoor pool and spa. A stone terrace across the south façade overlooks the great lawn which is enclosed by a brick retaining wall. The stone and half-timber façades were constructed with dressed stone masonry in the character of native "Wissahickon Schist", combined with pegged wood members infilled with stucco.

Other important details include a steeply-pitched Vermont black slate roof with cross-gable parapets, ornamental copper leader boxes and downspouts, brick chimney caps set in a Flemish bond pattern, and decorative limestone elements incorporated throughout. The wood doors and casement windows, including an oriel window on the north elevation, replicate the look of steel with narrow stiles and rails and are dressed with cut limestone surrounds. A collection of exterior structures includes two three-car garages, a garden loggia at the corner of the great lawn, a pergola overlook and ornamental wood gateways.

House 14,520 ft² (1349 m²)   Site 108 acres (44 ha)   Completion 2013

Interior designer KingsHaven Design   Contractor Pohlig Builders

Photography Joshua McHugh, Photographer

Previous pages The rear façade shows how the "L"- shaped plan was employed to facilitate linear interior circulation, provide each room with maximum exposure to exterior views and appropriately distribute the massing of major components.

These pages The first floor includes a grand entry hall, with plaster strapwork ceiling, stair hall, dining room, library, living room, kitchen, family room, orchid room and guest suite. The entry and mudroom doors were salvaged from a nearby Tudor Revival house, and historic light fixtures were salvaged and supplemented by original designs by KingsHaven Design.

Opposite Stair landing includes paneled walls with custom leaded glass cabinet doors. Above left and left Corner newel and stair hall show custom barley-turned oak balusters and newal posts inspired by Jacobean Revival precedent. Above Interior elevation and section detail show a hidden door concealed within the paneling.

Following pages from left to right Orchid room; Library detail; Outdoor fireplace in garden loggia.

NORMAN REVIVAL RESIDENCE

Near Philadelphia, Pennsylvania

This new residence in the French Norman Revival style is nestled into the landscape in a private setting near Philadelphia. The design of the exterior was inspired by the vernacular architecture of the French countryside. The home is organized around a walled garden courtyard with water features and a flanking loggia. The façades are constructed with dark red hand-molded brick laid with charcoal-color mortar and terra-cotta accents. The roof is clad in sculptural terra-cotta tile. Steel leaded-glass casement windows provide views of the sloping lawn and the ponds across the landscape.

The clients asked the architects to create a new residence with comfortable and refined living space on the first floor, and accommodations for visiting family members and guests on the second floor. Of particular importance was that the residence have a private setting, concealed from neighboring properties and thoroughfares and that the interiors have a diminutive scale. Interior spaces therefore are intimate in size and include custom-designed and finely-detailed woodwork with decorative plaster ceilings and quarter-sawn white oak flooring. The interior spatial organization is conducive to casual and relaxed living on one floor for the busy professional clients.

House 6000 ft² (557 m²)   **Site** 3.5 acres (1.42 ha)   **Completion** 2008
Landscape architect Jonathan Alderson Landscape Architects   **Contractor** E.B. Mahoney Builders, Inc.
Photography Don Pearse Photographers Inc.; Tom Crane Photography

Previous pages The secluded and sloped site contains existing mature specimen trees and a narrow stream serving two small inter-connected ponds. Terraces were designed as extensions of the house and landscaping complements the home in texture and evolving seasonal color.
Above left Side entry door to garage loggia, featuring wrought-iron strap hinges and thumb latch. Above right Entry hall with barrel-vaulted ceiling and plaster-strapwork ceiling. Right Design for custom wrought-iron strapwork hinge. Opposite Family room features hand-hewn trusses and a marble mantel.

KINSLEY

Oxford, Maryland

Kinsley is a 150-acre (61-hectare) waterfront property in Oxford, Maryland. The design for the new residence was inspired by the early 18th-century architecture of Williamsburg while responding to the particular opportunities afforded by the site and the very personal perceptions of the clients. Of particular importance in the design and construction of this house was the celebration of 18th-century craftspeople who created their buildings with an innate understanding of design and proportion, and a profound respect for the legacy of their craft.

The interior spaces accommodate the formal fenestrations of the façades and incorporate traditional 18th-century elements of design, but are contemporary in their juxtaposition to support an informal lifestyle. On the first floor, the living room, dining room and kitchen face the water, while the foyer, stairway and family entrance space are arranged by an enfilade along the entrance façade. On the second floor, the master bedroom and related spaces face the water.

Although appearing somewhat monumental when first encountered, the residence is actually of a quite intimate scale, serving as a home for clients who share a life-long appreciation for 18th-century architecture and thrive on access to the benefits of life on the water.

House 3035 ft² (282 m²)   **Site** 150 acres (61 ha)   **Completion** 2015

Interior designer Barbara Gisel Design, Ltd.   **Contractor** Heim Corporation

Photography Don Pearse Photographers Inc.

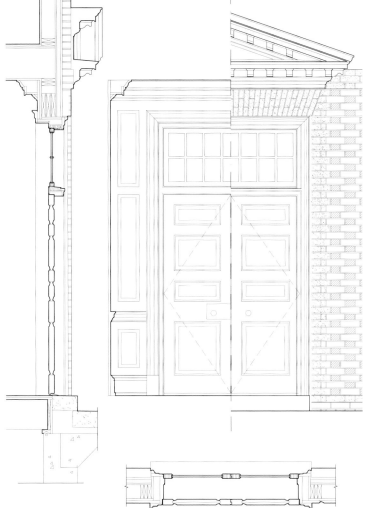

Opposite Shown between the home and detached garage, the view from three façades is of gardens with the water beyond.

Top left and left The exterior walls are constructed of hand-molded red brick laid with glazed headers set in a Flemish bond pattern with contrasting rubbed brick detailing. The window and door frames are of pegged mortise-and-tenon construction and interior woodwork has mortise-and-tenon joinery with hand-planed surfaces. The steeply pitched roof is clad in heavy cedar shakes. A one-story porch with flanking outdoor rooms is positioned on the water side. Above Front entrance detail.

Following pages clockwise from left View of dining area and kitchen beyond; View of entry hall through to the dining area; Kitchen; View from the dining area looking into the entry hall; View from the formal dining room showing fireplace with living room and stair hall beyond.

KEN TATE ARCHITECT

Architect Ken Tate describes himself as an intuitive classicist—two words rarely found in the same sentence. While the word intuitive speaks of imagination, unpredictability, and the creative unconscious, the term classicist implies an orderly, rational reliance upon the language of classical architecture. In the abstract, it is difficult to grasp this marriage of apparently contradictory modes, but when one walks through a house designed by Tate, the architect's meaning becomes quite clear. Pitch-perfect proportions, elegant enfilades (a suite of rooms with doorways in line with each other), and Classical columns lend order and calmness. Asymmetrical floor plans with rooms that shift from style to style, often moving from the formal to vernacular, create a relaxing, human environment.

"I love classicism, but I don't approach it in a rigid, academic way," explains Tate, whose creative process is never quite the same from project to project. Each residential design evolves in response to several elements, including the immediate site, the surrounding natural and architectural environment, and the aesthetic vision and physical needs of the clients. But the manner in which Tate travels from the beginning of each project to its conclusion is unique, shaped by intuition, imagination, and a bone-deep understanding of the language of architecture.

If a client requests a house in a specific style, such as Federal or country French, Tate enters into the spirit of the idiom in order to seek the right answers to questions, such as these: How can the house fit best within its surroundings? What specific materials and craftsmanship are required to invoke the sense of comfort or elegance associated with the style? What modifications are needed to suit the project?

Rather than approach these questions in a rational, "left-brain" manner while sitting at his drawing table, Tate prefers to employ what he describes as a kind of method acting. "I just get into the spirit of whatever style I'm working on at the moment, and go with what feels right, what would look as if it's always been there," the architect told a reporter from Clem Labine's *Period Homes* in 2000. According to Tate, the resulting houses "look familiar—but you couldn't necessarily find anything like them if you tried."

"When one follows one's intuition without any preconceived notions, one can arrive at a solution that feels right."

The New Old House

Nashville, Tennessee

This 10,000-square-foot (929-square-meter) residence in the historic
Belle Meade neighborhood of Nashville, Tennessee, invokes the concept of
vernacular progression— the manner in which houses grow and evolve over time.
Disparate parts of the dwelling resemble a vernacular Tennessee fieldstone barn,
a Georgian house, a Federal wing, and a Colonial Revival addition.

Thanks to Tate's attention to period-appropriate materials and craftsmanship, these
attached structures appear to have been built over two centuries. This approach
made it possible to design a large house accommodating the owners' modern needs,
while also complementing the style and scale of the surrounding Colonial Revival
dwellings. Although the house is significantly larger than those nearby, the manner in
which Tate divided the mass into smaller parts diminishes its appearance of size.

House 10,000 ft² (929 m²) **Site** 106,000 ft² (9848 m²) **Completion** 2004
Interior designer Erwin & White **Landscape architects** Charles Stick; Joseph Hodgson
Photography Timothy Dunford; Gordon Beall

Previous pages (left) The entrance door detailing is executed in a delicate Federal style, while the walls of the portico are wooden blocks beveled to resemble cut stone; (right) The delicate front door detailing appears on the interior side as well.

Opposite The Greek Revival breakfast room looks out over the verdant landscape through triple-hung windows "in-filled" between square-tapered Doric columns. Above left The formal dining room was "remodeled" in the Federal style within the America Colonial main house. Above right These Georgian arches beautifully express the intersection of two hallways.

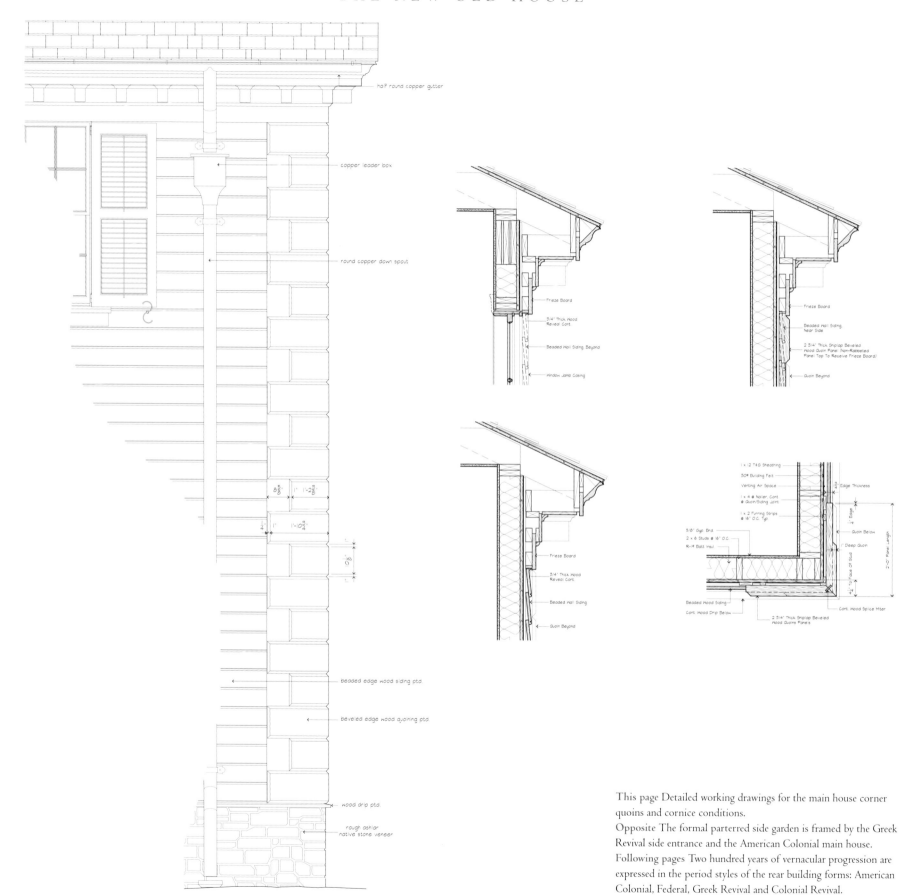

half round copper gutter

copper leader box

round copper down spout

Frieze Board

3/4" Thick Wood
Reveal Cont.

Beaded Wall Siding Beyond

Window Jamb Casing

Frieze Board

Beaded Wall Siding,
Rear Side

2 3/4" Thick Shiplap Beveled
Wood Quoin Panel (Non-Rabbeted
Panel Top To Receive Frieze Board)

Quoin Beyond

Frieze Board

3/4" Thick Wood
Reveal Cont.

Beaded Wall Siding

Quoin Beyond

1 x 12 T&G Sheathing

30# Building Felt

Venting Air Space

1 x 4 # Nailer Cont.
@ Quoin/Siding Joint

1 x 2 Furring Strips
@ 16" O.C. Typ.

5/8" Gyp. Brd.

2 x 6 Studs @ 16" O.C.

R-14 Batt Insul.

Edge Thickness

Edge

Quoin Below

Deep Quoin

To Face Of Stud

Panel Length

Beaded Wood Siding

Cont. Wood Drip Below

2 3/4" Thick Shiplap Beveled
Wood Quoin Panels

Cont. Wood Splice Miter

beaded edge wood siding ptd

beveled edge wood quoining ptd

wood drip ptd.

rough ashlar
native stone veneer

This page Detailed working drawings for the main house corner quoins and cornice conditions.

Opposite The formal parterred side garden is framed by the Greek Revival side entrance and the American Colonial main house.

Following pages Two hundred years of vernacular progression are expressed in the period styles of the rear building forms: American Colonial, Federal, Greek Revival and Colonial Revival.

An Urban Villa

New Orleans, Louisiana

Combining classical elements inspired by the architecture of Andrea Palladio with those recalling the romantic character of the Mediterranean Revival, this 12,800-square-foot (1189-square-meter) house pays homage to and enhances the extraordinary streetscape of New Orleans' Saint Charles Avenue. Inspired by Palladio's Basilica in Vicenza, the façade features a single-story portico with a cut-stone arcade and a balustrade terrace above. Offset by the overall simplicity of the façade, the portico's effect is dramatic without overshadowing the surrounding architecture. Located on a corner, the house has a secondary façade with picturesque Mediterranean Revival features, including iron gates, a second-story pergola, and a tower. Accommodating the clients' art collection, Ken Tate's interior plan combines smooth plaster walls and simple casings with adorned ceilings, including groin and barrel vaults, beams, and paneling.

House 12,800 ft² (1189 m²) **Site** 27,000 ft² (2508 m²) **Completion** 2016
Interior designer Gerrie Bremermann **Landscape architect** Gavin Duke (Page/Duke Landscape Architects)
Photography Timothy Dunford; Fred Licht

Previous pages (left) The front portico is based on a Palladian order of columns, pilasters, arches, and plaster groin vaults. The lanterns are cast bronze. (right) A view from the steps of the front portico through the open front doors and on through the house to the rear loggia and garden beyond. Above The view from the entrance hall through the open front doors to the front gates and St. Charles Avenue beyond. The stone paving has a pattern of black onyx cabochons. Right The living room has smooth plaster walls and limed antique oak beams with carved classical brackets.

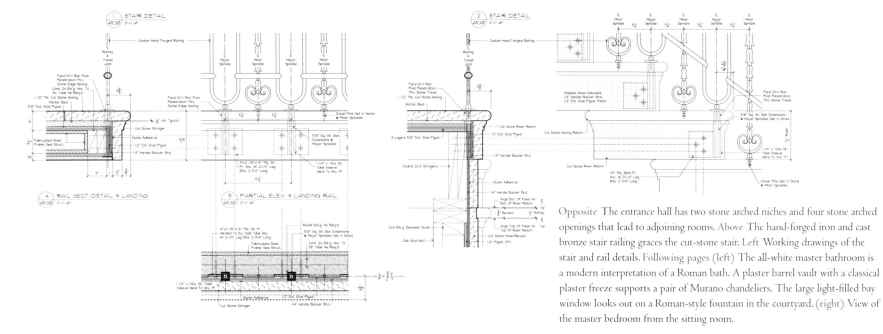

Opposite The entrance hall has two stone arched niches and four stone arched openings that lead to adjoining rooms. Above The hand-forged iron and cast bronze stair railing graces the cut-stone stair. Left Working drawings of the stair and rail details. Following pages (left) The all-white master bathroom is a modern interpretation of a Roman bath. A plaster barrel vault with a classical plaster freeze supports a pair of Murano chandeliers. The large light-filled bay window looks out on a Roman-style fountain in the courtyard. (right) View of the master bedroom from the sitting room.

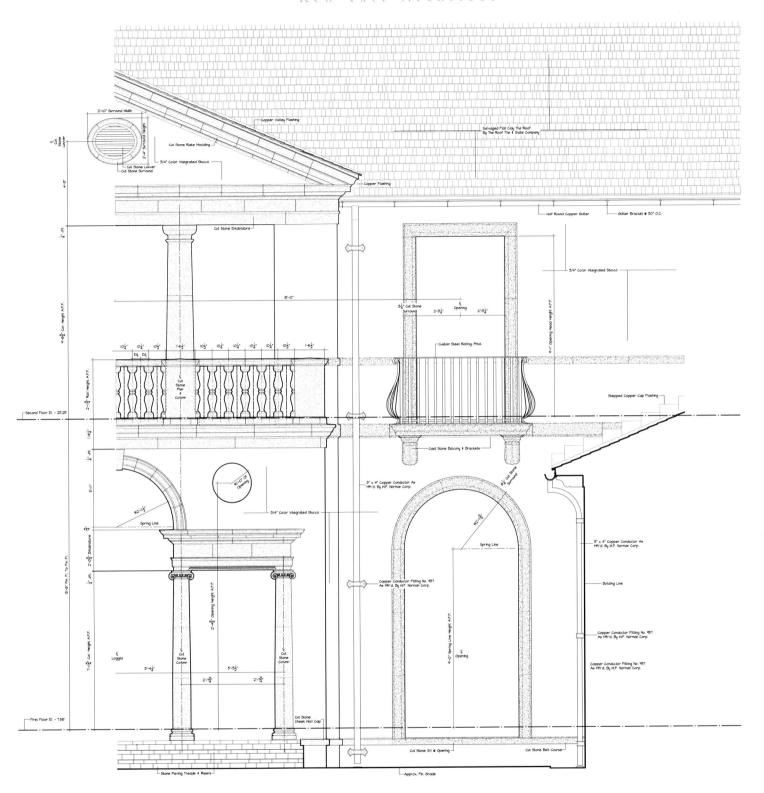

Opposite The rear loggia is a grand space intended for both family gatherings, as well as for large numbers of guests. The steel doors and windows on the left are along the length of the interior gallery. The doors straight ahead lead into the master bedroom sitting area. Above A detailed working drawing elevation of the rear central portion of the main house. The second-floor rear loggia is shown here over the first-floor loggia.

Previous pages (left) This Ionic Palladian cut-stone opening beautifully frames the courtyard garden and pool area.
A Roman-style fountain is the centerpiece of the space, while a Roman fountain mask provides a classical terminus.
(right) An oasis in the city. Here the deep blue pool, with potted lemon trees at each corner, is flanked by the pool house
on the left and the master bedroom wing (and pergola) on the right. A Roman fountain and pedimented loggias beyond
remind us we are in a classical Italian space. Opposite This courtyard view reveals the second-floor pedimented loggia with
Doric columns surmounting the first-floor loggia with an Ionic Palladian opening (only partially shown). The tower beyond
anchors the space to the outside world. The lawn was designed for future tented parties with Roman fountain as the tent's
centerpiece. Above The side street entry and guest parking is anchored by the classical Italian tower and the more vernacular
farmhouse "stable" on the right. The pergola / balcony over the side entry has doors to the media room.

A Colonial Revival Estate

Nashville, Tennessee

This 12,000-square-foot (1115-square-meter) house in Nashville, Tennessee, is a modern interpretation of the creative eclecticism of the Colonial Revival period. Employing the formality of 1930s Federal Revival architecture in the scored stucco-over-brick portico and arcade-like side wing, Tate expressed a wider range of references within. A Georgian-inspired great hall with a cantilevered staircase rises in the center of the house. This hall leads to formal dining room with stately Georgian moldings and an Adamesque drawing room. In the kitchen and family dining room, painted paneling and cross-beam ceilings recall mid-twentieth century Colonial Revival interiors. Blending elegance with informality, Tate designed a family living room wing that marries a high-style Palladian doorway and rustic standing-seam copper roof without with Georgian paneling and primitive timber-frame ceiling trusses within.

House 12,000 ft² (1115 m²)   **Site** 77,537 ft² (7203 m²)   **Completion** 2006
Interior designer Landy Gardner   **Landscape architect** Page/Duke
Photography Timothy Dunford

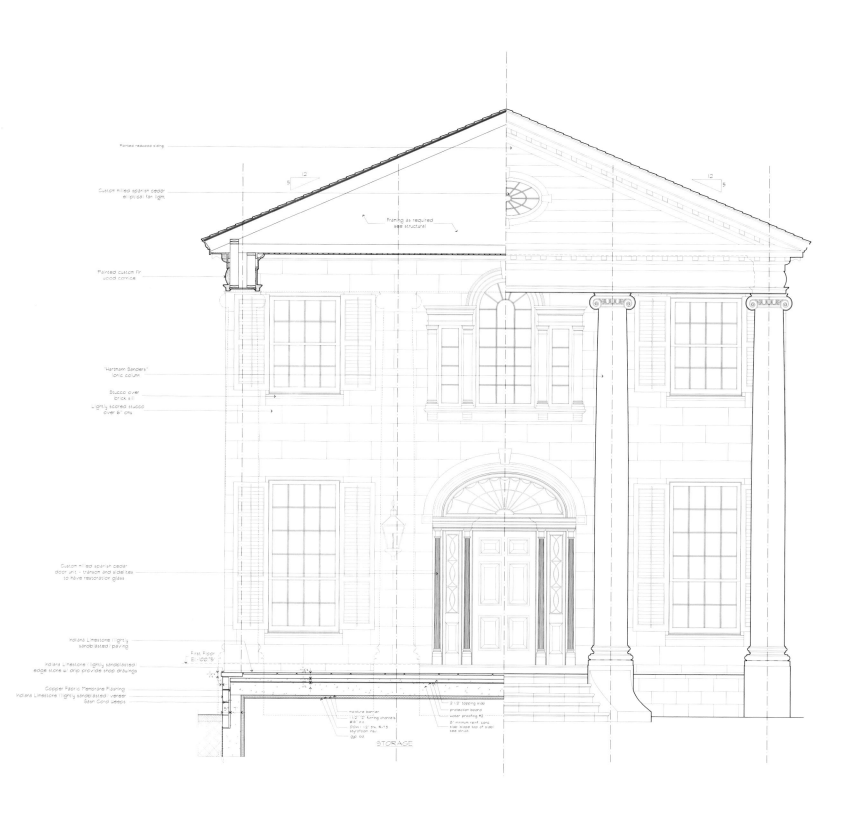

Painted redwood siding

Custom milled spanish cedar
elliptical fan light

Framing as required
see structural

Painted custom fir
wood cornice

"Hartmann Sanders"
Ionic column

Stucco over
brick sill

Lightly scored stucco
over 8" cmu

Custom milled spanish cedar
door unit - transom and sidelites
to have restoration glass

Indiana Limestone (lightly
sandblasted) paving

First Floor
EL. 100'-0"

Indiana Limestone (lightly sandblasted)
edge stone w/ drip provide shop drawings

Copper Fabric Membrane Flashing
Indiana Limestone (lightly sandblasted) veneer
Sash Cord Weeps

moisture barrier
1/2" "Z" furring channels
@16" o.c.
Down 1-1/2" thk. R-13
styrofoam insul.
gyp. bd.

2 1/2" topping slab
protection board
water proofing #2
8" minimum reinf. conc.
slab - slope top of slab
see struct

STORAGE

Previous pages (left) This working drawing of the front portico shows one half with the columns and pediment in front of the wall of the house and one half with those removed in order to show the Palladian window and the full extent of the plaster scoring. (right) Delicate wood tracery was used for the front-door transom and sidelights. The wall of the portico has scored stucco to resemble cut-stone—a practice that was used in the American, Georgian, and Federal periods.

Opposite The entrance hall is square and is also symmetrical on two axes, which allows a square vaulted plaster groin vault to spring from a low cornice that is tangent to the spring line of four elliptical arches. Above left The central stair hall's two-story spaciousness is beautifully expressed by a Georgian cantilevered wooden stair. The risers are articulated as three-dimensional painted wood paneled boxes, while the railings are made of walnut and finished like furniture. Above right The stair hall's second-floor landing has a false lantern that is actually built into the attic (the light comes from skylights on the roof!). This was done for its architectural effect.

Following pages (left) The rear Ionic portico, with its Chippendale railing, frames a view of the pavilion-like family room. Two large Palladian windows (one on each side of the room) and the glass cupola allow ample natural light into the antique timber-framed family room with painted paneling. (right) The rear of the house shows the "added-on" Greek Revival pool house on the left and the Federal main house straight ahead.

A Bahamian Compound

New Providence, Bahamas

An authentic British Colonial house sited on a peninsula with panoramic water views, this 8000-square-foot (743-square-meter) estate in Old Fort, New Providence, captures the charm of colonial Bahamian style—a marriage of stately Georgian architecture with Caribbean simplicity. With perfect symmetry and a classical portico, the façade has a Georgian aesthetic, but white stucco, wood shingles, and uncomplicated details are Bahamian in flavor. Like early island dwellings, the main block and wings are only one room deep, allowing breezes to flow throughout. Diverging from the formality of the façade, the wings are expressed in the local dialect with Bahamian prop shutters and tray ceilings that enhance air circulation. The beauty of the house stems from its blending of classical elegance with the purity of vernacular material and functional form.

House 8000 ft² (743 m²)   **Site** 59,500 ft² (552 8 m²)   **Completion** 2015
Interior designer David Kleinberg   **Landscape designer** Ken Tate
Photography Timothy Dunford

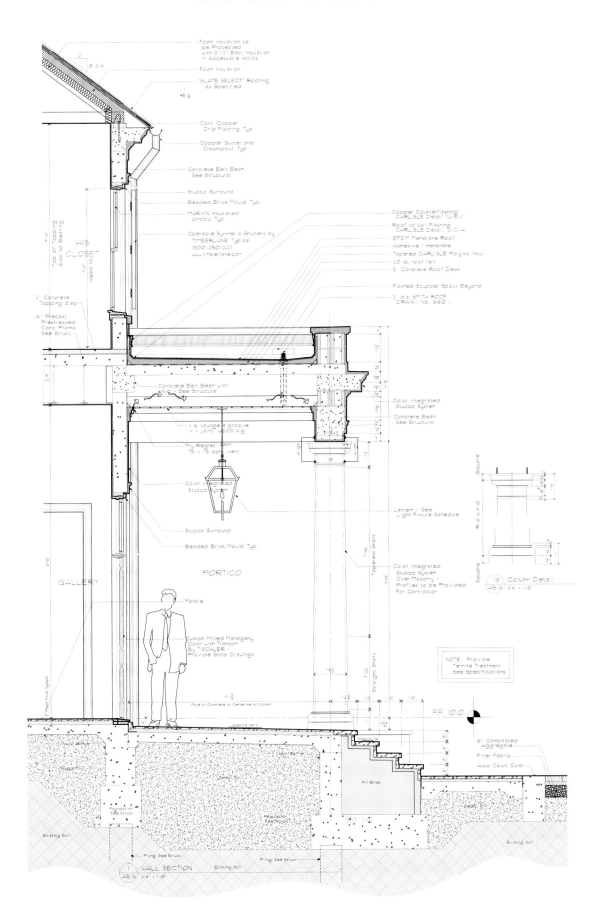

Foam Insulation to
be Protected
with 3 1/2" Batt Insulation
in Accessible Attics

Foam Insulation

"SLATE SELECT" Roofing
as Specified

Cont. Copper
Drip Flashing Typ.

Copper Gutter and
Downspout Typ.

Concrete Belt Beam
See Structural

Stucco Surround

Beaded Brick Mould Typ.

MARVIN Insulated
Window Typ.

Operable Synthetic Shutters by
TIMBERLANE Typical
1-800-250-2221
www.timberlane.com

Copper Counterflashing
CARLISLE Detail "U-3-J

Roof to Wall Flashing
CARLISLE Detail "U-2-A"

EPDM Membrane Roof

Adhesive Membrane

Tapered CARLISLE Polyiso Insul.

30 lb. roof felt

5" Concrete Roof Deck

Flashed Scupper Spout Beyond

3" dia. SMITH ROOF
DRAIN (No. 1660)

2" Concrete
Topping Slab

6" Precast
Prestressed
Conc. Planks
See Struct.

Concrete Belt Beam with
Nib. See Structural

Color Integrated
Stucco System

Concrete Beam
See Structural

1 x 6 tongue & groove
V - joint - Wood c.g.

Dry Reglet
"8 x 8 conc. vent

Color Integrated
Stucco System

Lantern - See
Light Fixture Schedule

Stucco Surround

Beaded Brick Mould Typ.

Color Integrated
Stucco System
Over Masonry -
Profiles to be Provided
For Contractor

PORTICO

GALLERY

Marble

Custom Milled Mahogany
Door with Transom
By TISCHLER -
Provide Shop Drawings

NOTE: Provide
Termite Treatment
See Specifications

FF 100.0

Column Detail

6" Compacted
Aggregate

Filter Fabric

Auto Court Curb

Face of Concrete to Centerline of Column

Foundation
See Struct.

Footing See Struct.

Existing Soil

WALL SECTION

Fill Brick

Previous pages (left) The main house is a Colonial Georgian style built of stucco over masonry to withstand frequent hurricanes in the Bahamas. (right) The working drawing section through the front portico and two-story wall.
Above left The front entrance gallery has Georgian elements: checkerboard stone paving, a coved plaster ceiling, and arched openings. Above right This view from the entrance gallery into the living room reveals a carved stone Georgian mantle and a painted wood coffered ceiling. Opposite The living room has a relaxed island feeling, while still adhering to the Georgian style.
Following pages (left) A large grouping of French doors and transoms allows a beautiful view through the rear veranda to the pool, canal and mango grove beyond. (right) The rear veranda has a 14-foot (4.27-meter) ceiling height, French limestone paving, stucco over masonry classical columns, direct access to the pool and a magnificent view of the water beyond.

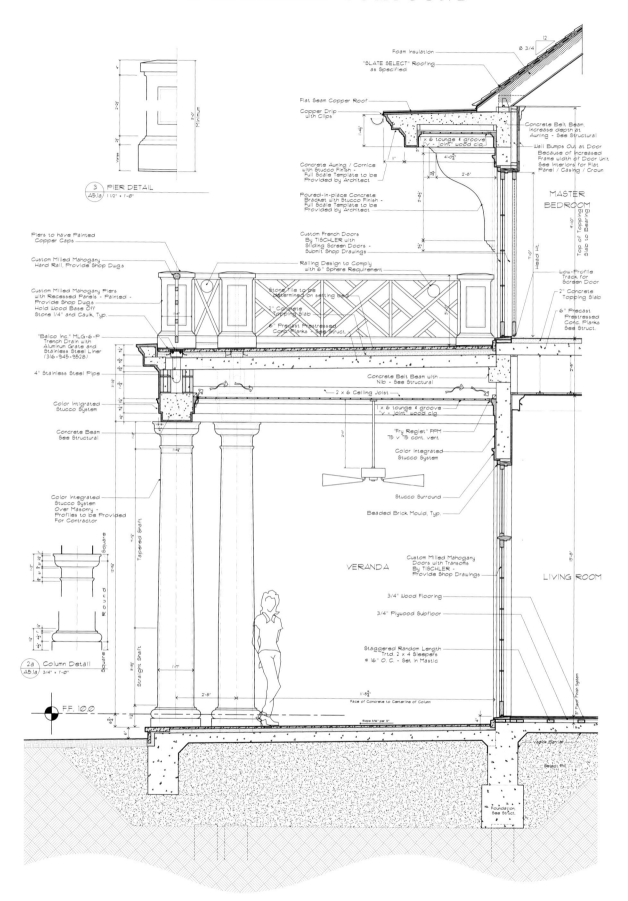

Foam Insulation

"SLATE SELECT" Roofing
as Specified

8 3/4
12

Flat Seam Copper Roof

Copper Drip
with Clips

Concrete Belt Beam -
Increase depth at
Awning - See Structural

1 x 6 tongue & groove
"v - joint" wood clg.

Wall Bumps Out at Door
Because of Increased
Frame Width of Door Unit
See Interiors for Flat
Panel / Casing / Crown

MASTER
BEDROOM

Concrete Awning / Cornice
with Stucco Finish -
Full Scale Template to be
Provided by Architect

Poured-in-place Concrete
Bracket with Stucco Finish -
Full Scale Template to be
Provided by Architect

Custom French Doors
By TISCHLER with
Sliding Screen Doors -
Submit Shop Drawings

Piers to have Painted
Copper Caps

Custom Milled Mahogany
Hand Rail, Provide Shop Dwgs.

Railing Design to Comply
with 6" Sphere Requirement

Low-Profile
Track for
Screen Door

Custom Milled Mahogany Piers
with Recessed Panels - Painted -
Provide Shop Dwgs
Hold Wood Base Off
Stone 1/4" and Caulk, Typ.

Stone Tile to be
Determined on setting bed

2" Concrete
Topping Slab

2" Concrete
Topping Slab

6" Precast
Prestressed
Conc. Planks
See Struct.

6" Precast Prestressed
Conc. Planks - See Struct.

"Balco Inc." MLG-6-P
Trench Drain with
Aluminum Grate and
Stainless Steel Liner
(316-345-9528)

Concrete Belt Beam with
Nib - See Structural

4" Stainless Steel Pipe

2 x 6 Ceiling Joist

1 x 6 tongue & groove
"v - joint" wood clg.

Color Intigrated
Stucco System

"Fry Reglet" FFM
15 v 15 cont. vent

Concrete Beam
See Structural

Color Integrated
Stucco System

Color Integrated
Stucco System
Over Masonry -
Profiles to be Provided
For Contractor

Stucco Surround

Beaded Brick Mould, Typ.

VERANDA

Custom Milled Mahogany
Doors with Transoms
By TISCHLER -
Provide Shop Drawings

LIVING ROOM

3/4" Wood Flooring

3/4" Plywood Subfloor

Staggered Random Length
Trtd. 2 x 4 Sleepers
@ 16" O.C. - Set in Mastic

F.F. 10.0

Face of Concrete to Centerline of Column

Foundation
See Struct.

3 PIER DETAIL
A5.la | 1 1/2" = 1'-0"

2a Column Detail
A5.la | 3/4" = 1'-0"

Previous pages (left) A working drawing section through the living room's veranda and the master bedroom's terrace above. (right) The rear veranda (with the master bedroom terrace above) and the kitchen / family room porch (with a bedroom porch above) share the pool with the pool house beyond.

Left This night view of the house from the large expansive rear lawn reveals how every room (and some minor rooms) have great views of the water.

SMITH
ARCHITECTURAL GROUP

As a child growing up in Chicago, Jeffery Smith was surrounded by the work of such great American architects as Frank Lloyd Wright and Louis Sullivan. When he moved to Palm Beach as a teen the influence of noted architects Addison Mizner and Maurice Fatio continued to illuminate his interest not only in architecture but in the architecture that creates a house.

Houses of the scale that Smith builds are almost always designed for a client and the whole process of creating "for" someone has its own challenges and merits. Smith's firm prides itself on rigorous execution. If a client is interested in a specific style, that style is executed with an impeccable eye for the details and the firm will guide a client to make informed decisions so that the purity is maintained. Every element is carefully thought out, weighed and integrated, leaving nothing to chance with ideas sometimes morphing in a very organic way as the house rises out of the ground taking on a life of its own. While architecture can be theoretical the practice is what makes it come alive.

Smith's floor plans are structured, sequenced for the experience. The scale of the formal rooms is grand without being overwhelming and the private rooms are intimate but still gracious. The plan informs the elevations, but the elevations themselves are typically formal, tightly constructed classical façades that stay true to their style.

Smith has an avid interest in preservation and many of his projects are restorations to landmark structures. This admiration of the old is evidenced through the new construction where sometimes it is difficult to differentiate. "The greatest compliment we can receive is when someone walks into one of our new houses and thinks it was a restoration," Smith says.

Despite the formality, Smith's houses are comfortable, livable. The subtlety of the details unfolds in layers from the grand scale to the minute as you move through the spaces. Within the rigidity though there is room for whimsy: column capitals stylized with dolphins that reflect the nearby ocean, seahorse brackets elegantly craning their necks to hold the balcony above. These elements take the classical orders and add a signature twist that makes them unique. Creating classical architecture is not a merely a regurgitation of what has come before but is a library of knowledge to be referenced, interpreted and implemented in a thoughtful and cohesive way.

"We are traditionalists who design in a timeless style.
We endeavor to make a new house look like you inherited it."

Serenity

Palm Beach, Florida

Serenity is located on the idyllic island of Palm Beach with its rich history of stately homes. The art of architecture sometimes requires adapting a traditional style to its surrounding environment. This was true in the design of Serenity. A Georgian style of architecture was adapted to accommodate a subtropical climate.

Serenity sits proudly on its site like its countless Georgian predecessors, however, this house, like the earlier Georgian houses of the tropics, has a more casual approach in the use of the materials and colors employed. Stone and brick have been replaced with stucco and the buttery yellow façade, although in contrast to the typical Georgian palette, is reflective of a balmier climate. Classic Georgian details are evidenced in the use of the Doric and Ionic columns, arch surrounds and the broken pediment façade. Cast stone balustrade and column plinths adhere to the strict classical proportion of the ancient Greeks and Romans and the Palladian detailing is a recurring theme on the façades.

House 25,000 ft² (2323 m²) **Site** 65,000 ft² (6039 m²) **Completion** 2002

Interior designers David Easton and Eric Smith **Landscape architects** Madison Cox Associates

Photography Sargent Architectural Photography

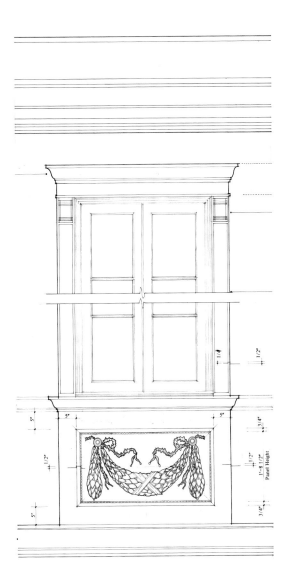

Left The entry façade is detailed with Doric columns, rusticated base and broken pedimented roof. Above Detail drawing of the windows. Following pages (left) The classical interiors are flawlessly executed by David Easton and Eric Smith. (right) The stair foyer and gallery beyond are lavishly appointed with classical details.

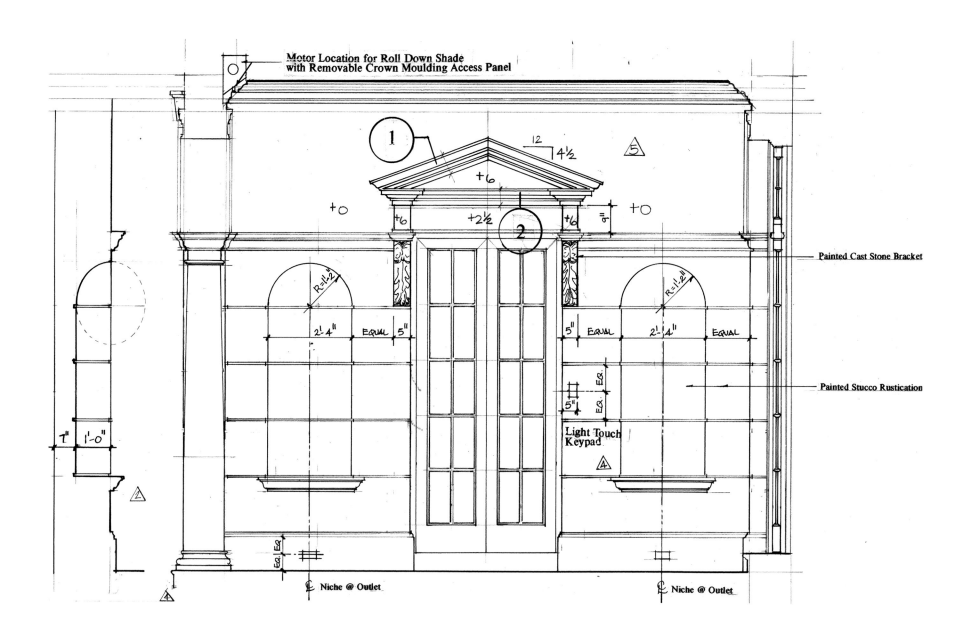

Motor Location for Roll Down Shade
with Removable Crown Moulding Access Panel

Painted Cast Stone Bracket

Painted Stucco Rustication

Light Touch
Keypad

Niche @ Outlet

Niche @ Outlet

Above Detail drawings of the loggia showing a section of the niche (left) and the north elevation (right).
Opposite The rustication and Doric columns continue into the lake loggia at the rear façade.
Following pages The house is a modified H plan and allows expansive water views from all major rooms of the house.
The "legs" of the H encapsulate a large loggia with covered terrace above, creating a courtyard effect. The loggia and
terrace help blur the distinction between the interior and exterior while simultaneously shielding the intense Florida sun.

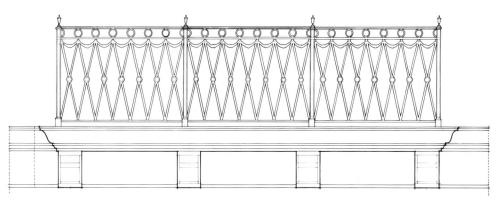

Top A view of the dining room from the exterior, featuring oeil-de-boeuf windows and balcony above. Above Façade detail drawing of the balcony. Right While the house does incorporate the traditional elements of Georgian architecture—proportion, symmetry, overtures to Palladian architecture—it also contradicts some of the traditional norms. Serenity has a distinctly greater ratio of fenestration to building mass. The result is a lighter, airier, more feminine version of its English counterpart that allows for more interaction with the outdoors than the traditional Georgian prototype. The view here is of the rear façade as seen from the pool.

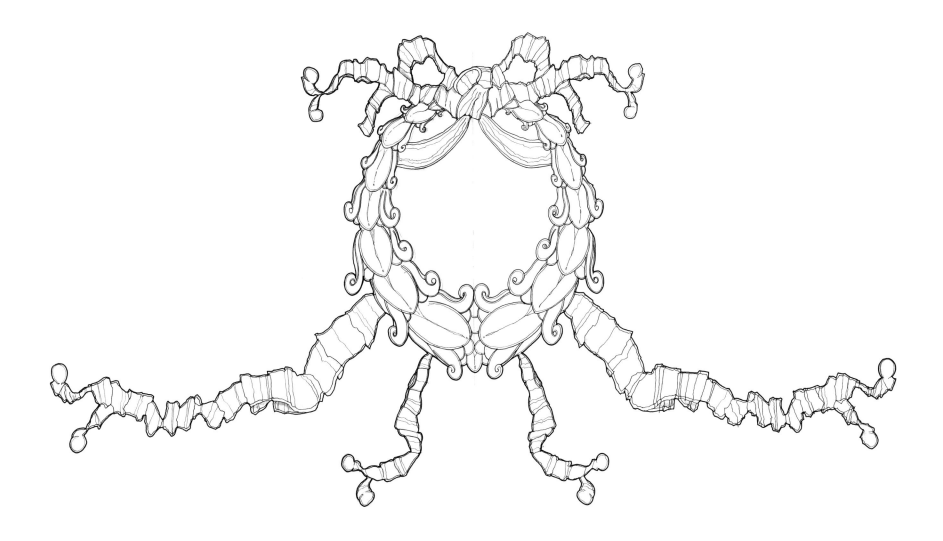

Opposite The guest house sits on a cross axis with the main residence. It stands alone as a little jewel box next to its
more formidable counterpart and faces south to capture views down the intracoastal waterway. Although smaller in scale,
it compliments the massing of the main residence by sharing its detailing and proportion.
Above Drawing detail of the cartouche.

Villa Penguinos

Indian Creek Island, Florida

Villa Penguinos is a 27,000-square-foot (2508-square-meter) residence situated on Indian Creek Island in Biscayne Bay near Miami, Florida. The almost 2-acre (0.75-hectare) pie-shaped parcel allows for the main residence to sit back from the street on a manicured lawn, with room for gracious terraces, pool and pavilions.

Villa Penguinos draws its inspiration from Palladio, and, like Palladian villas of the past, takes into account the site and its views. The house sits upon a stone plinth creating an imposing and more guarded view from the street. The fenestrations on the façade are small, punched openings and the two single-story wings reach out to symmetrically frame the motor court and entry portico. As the site opens toward the bay, so does the house. The façade facing the bay is more open and lighter. On the ground floor all of the main rooms have extensive views of the water, as do all of the main bedroom suites on the second floor.

The wide lot allows for all of the main rooms to not only face the water but also be interconnected by loggias, creating a rhythm of solid and void along the rear façade.

House 27,000 ft² (2508 m²) **Site** 80,000 ft² (7432 m²) **Completion** 2009

Landscape architect Nievera Williams

Photography Sargent Architectural Photography

Left The view of the formal entry from the motor court.
Above Detail drawing of the wrought-iron entry door.

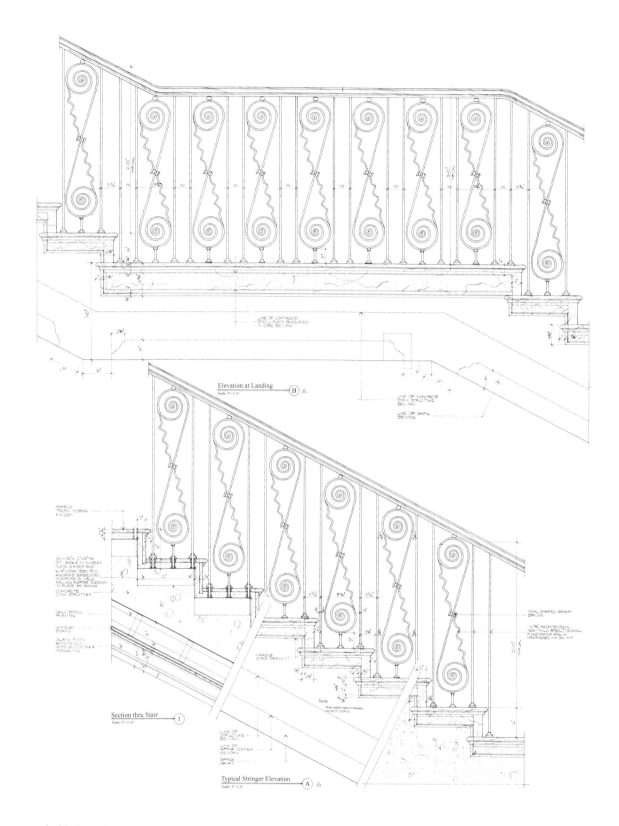

Elevation at Landing (B)
Scale: 3"=1'-0"

Section thru Stair (1)
Scale: 3"=1'-0"

Typical Stringer Elevation (A)
Scale: 3"=1'-0"

Note

Left The main rooms are highly detailed with classical ornamentation—the curved stair in the foyer (which leads to the main gallery) has intricate wrought-iron railings, carved stone arches frame the main gallery and living room beyond, and coffered ceilings are featured throughout the main rooms. Above Detail drawings of the iron railing.

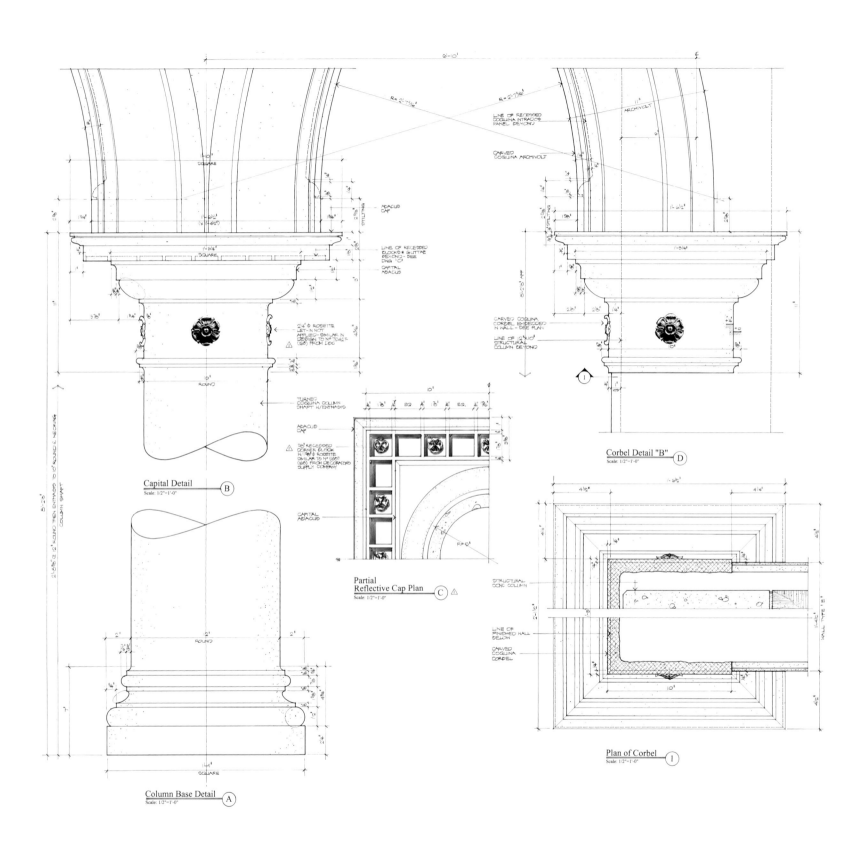

Capital Detail (B)
Scale: 1/2"=1'-0"

Partial
Reflective Cap Plan (C)
Scale: 1/2"=1'-0"

Corbel Detail "B" (D)
Scale: 1/2"=1'-0"

Column Base Detail (A)
Scale: 1/2"=1'-0"

Plan of Corbel (I)
Scale: 1/2"=1'-0"

Above Detail drawings of the carved stone columns.
Right Detail of the underside of the carved abacus cap.

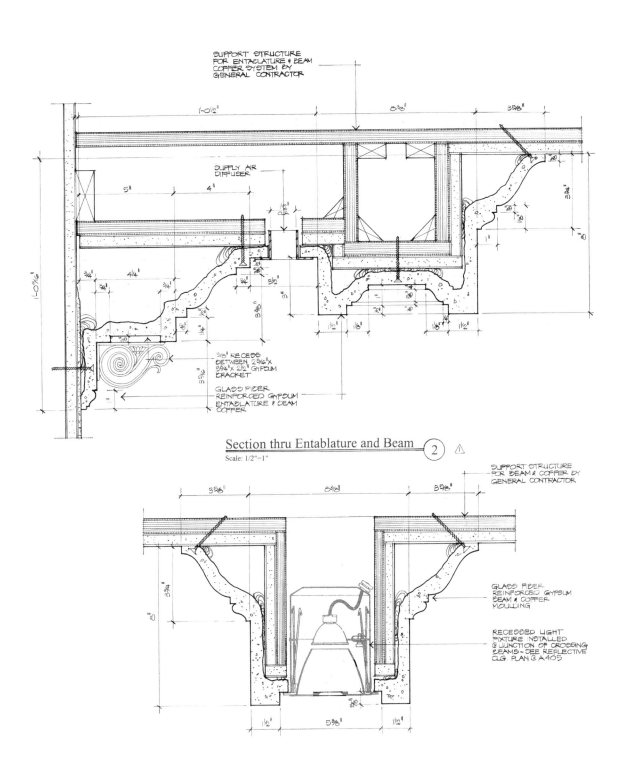

SUPPORT STRUCTURE
FOR ENTABLATURE & BEAM
COPPER SYSTEM BY
GENERAL CONTRACTOR

SUPPLY AIR
DIFFUSER

3/8" RECESS
BETWEEN 2%" X
3¾" X 2½" GYPSUM
BRACKET

GLASS FIBER
REINFORCED GYPSUM
ENTABLATURE & BEAM
COPPER

Section thru Entablature and Beam ② ⚠

Scale: 1/2"=1"

SUPPORT STRUCTURE
FOR BEAM & COPPER BY
GENERAL CONTRACTOR

GLASS FIBER
REINFORCED GYPSUM
BEAM & COPPER
MOULDING

RECESSED LIGHT
FIXTURE INSTALLED
@ JUNCTION OF CROSSING
BEAMS ~ SEE REFLECTIVE
CLG. PLAN @ A405

Above Detail section drawings of the coffer ceiling.
Right The living room has a sophisticated neutral palette.

276

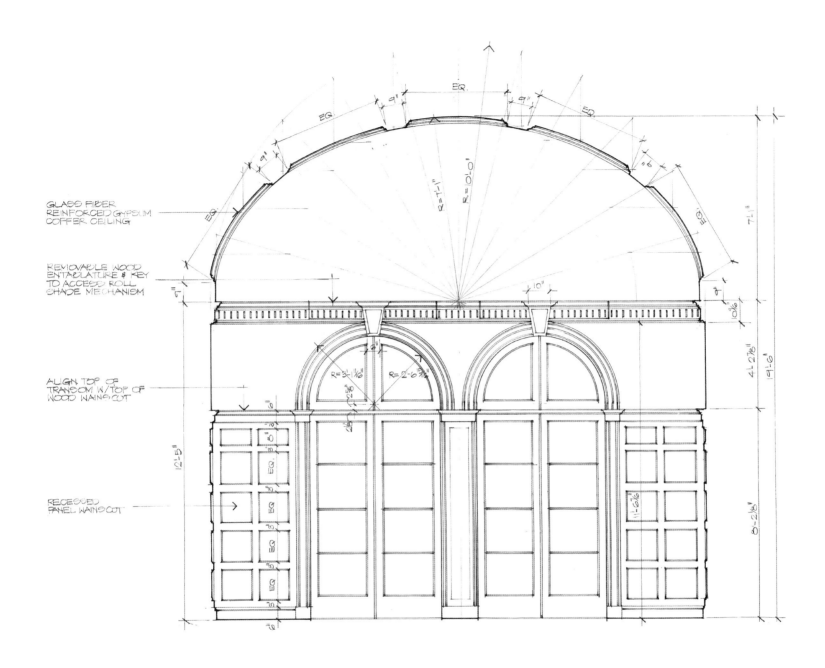

GLASS FIBER
REINFORCED GYPSUM
COFFER CEILING

REMOVABLE WOOD
ENTABLATURE & KEY
TO ACCESS ROLL
SHADE MECHANISM

ALIGN TOP OF
TRANSOM W/TOP OF
WOOD WAINSCOT

RECESSED
PANEL WAINSCOT

EQ.

EQ.

EQ.

EQ.

Opposite The elegant billiard room is adorned with parquet de Versailles flooring,
oak paneling, and an elliptical plaster-coffered ceiling.
Above Detail drawing of the south elevation of the billard room.

Above The main loggia has an elaborate mosaic floor and coffered ceiling. Right On the water side at the rear façade, the stone plinth gives way to cascading terraces that escort you to the pool.
Following pages An allée of date palms frames the dining pavilion at one end of the pool. These jewel-like pavilions, which flank the pool, are reminiscent of Palladian-style temples. The pavilions are complementary in their design, one is enclosed and one is open, and their symmetry is reflected across the water of the pool.

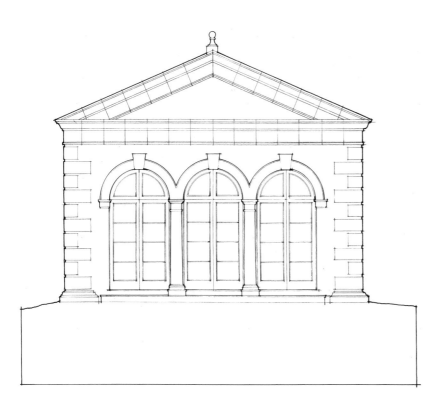

Above East elevation of the spa pavillon.
Right The pool terrace sits over 6 feet (1.8 meters) higher than the seawall,
allowing commanding views of the water and the Miami skyline.

La Tonteria

Palm Beach, Florida

La Tonteria is a landmark Georgian Revival home designed in 1935 by John L. Volk that commands an entire block at the north end of the island of Palm Beach.
The original plan of the residence was an "L" shape, but it had suffered from many renovations and had lost its original character and detail.

A pool cabana that had been added in the 1980s was removed to make way for a new addition that changed the plan to a "U," creating a courtyard between the wings. A new second story was also added to the west of the entry portico to balance the main façade.

Georgian architectural details were added to the entry foyer, main stair and living room to reinforce the original style of the home. The elegant oval stair was reversed to improve the flow to the library and a metal railing with gold swag detail and ram's heads was added. On the second floor, rooms were reconfigured so that the master bedroom was centered on the original east-facing balcony pediment. The master suite was expanded in both directions for his and her bathrooms and closets. The original sleeping porch spanning the second floor above the loggia was restored.

House 27,000 ft² (2508 m²)   **Site** 57,000 ft² (5295 m²)   **Completion** 2009
Interior designer Katherine Shenaman Interiors **Landscape architect** Nievera Williams Design
Photography Aerial Photography; Andy Frame; Steven Leeks; Jeffery W. Smith

Previous pages The main entry façade.
Above The foyer elevation on axis with the entry door.
Left An octagon coffered-plaster ceiling and leaded glass elliptical transom in the entry vestibule.

These pages The main stair railing with a stylized Ionic
balustrade that's adorned with ram's heads and ropes
with tassels.

Opposite (top) The dining room's walls are 17th-century Chinoiserie panels depicting the seasons, with a pagoda-style panel over the door that conceals air conditioning in the dining room. (bottom) The library features an antique French-oak paneling with shell motif. Above The living room features French doors to the terrace, new paneling and an antique mantel.

Following pages The family stair railing features three different pickets in an alternating design.

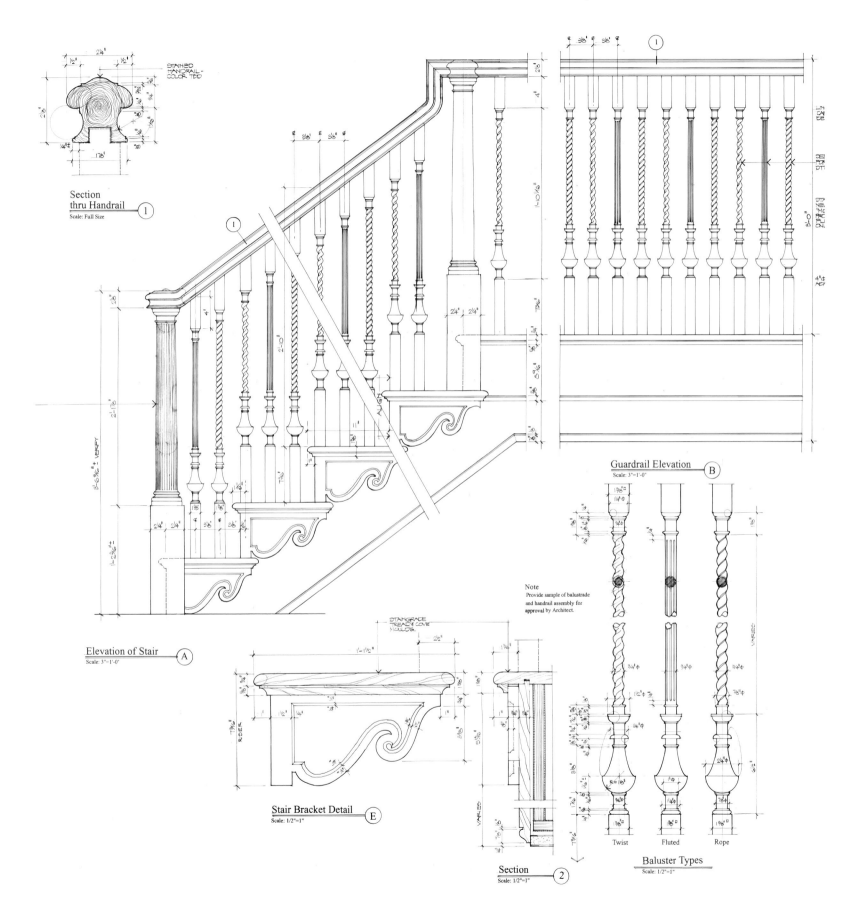

Section
thru Handrail   1
Scale: Full Size

STAINED
HANDRAIL -
COLOR TBD

Elevation of Stair   A
Scale: 3"=1'-0"

Stair Bracket Detail   E
Scale: 1/2"=1"

STAIR GRADE
TREAD & COVE
MOULDING.

Section   2
Scale: 1/2"=1"

Guardrail Elevation   B
Scale: 3"=1'-0"

Note
Provide sample of balustrade
and handrail assembly for
approval by Architect.

Twist   Fluted   Rope

Baluster Types
Scale: 1/2"=1"

Above The exterior façade overlooking the oceanside.
Opposite The courtyard and loggia beyond as seen from the swimming pool.

TIMOTHY BRYANT ARCHITECT

Timothy Bryant Architect, PLLC, is an award-winning, full-service architectural and design firm renowned for creating residences that celebrate craftsmanship, beauty, and a sense of place. Each of their projects is a balance of traditional and modern, influenced by classicism but designed for contemporary living through comprehensive consultations with a client to determine their particular dreams and visions for a home.

Timothy Bryant was born and raised in Windsor and High Wycombe, England, where he was immersed in architecture and the building arts from an early age through his father, a builder. A classicist by training with a background in interior design, Bryant has over 30 years of experience in the architecture and design field. He moved to the United States when he was twenty-one, and spent time exploring the architecture and landscape of the West Coast before eventually settling in New York City. Over the course of his career has had the opportunity to work with a number of other prominent architects and interior designers, including Thierry Despont, Ferguson & Shamamian, John Murray, Victoria Hagan, Mario Buatta, and Timothy Whealon.

Timothy Bryant finds inspiration everywhere—art, literature, nature, the landscape of the city—and seamlessly blends details from different time periods into each of his projects, making them feel modern and fresh while maintaining the soulfulness and patina that come from historical context. Bryant's client-oriented approach involves collaboration and partnership with a number of talented artisans, contractors and consultants who share his passion for craftsmanship and attention to detail.

The firm offers a wide range of services, including ground-up construction, restoration and renovation, historic preservation, property and site master planning, interior decoration and furniture planning, and adaptive reuse. They collaborate with a host of professionals—including artisans and craftspeople, preservationists and interior designers—to ensure that each element of the design is fully realized to the client's satisfaction, and they integrate sustainability and energy efficiency into homes through time-tested construction methods and fine materials.

The practice was formed in 1997 and has subsequently won a number of architecture and design awards. It has developed a reputation for a rare ability to translate a wide variety of architectural idioms into timeless residences that suit each of their client's particular needs and visions. Bryant is endlessly curious, which makes him a natural explorer of the past.

""A beautiful home has a sense of timelessness to it. No matter the style or size, you want a home to have a feeling of permanence."

A Home in Mandeville Canyon

Mandeville Canyon, California

The assignment for the project and property was to renovate and update the guest house, pool house, and tennis pavilion, but completely demolish the main house and rebuild it with a flowing plan and dedicated programming to suit the owner's needs. A new gate house was also to be added. Timothy Bryant worked with Victoria Hagan to develop a vision for blending the local vernacular of other homes in the area with an East Coast mood, thereby creating a unique, but appropriate character.

The owners and interior designer were heavily involved in all aspects of the planning and detailing, and their main goal was to create a unified master plan, assembling a small group of buildings that looked like they had naturally developed over time, but had been there a long time.

The final result was a dwelling with a special sense of place, at once unique and familiar, different from nearby Los Angeles, but well suited to its surroundings.

House 18,000 ft² (1672 m²) Site 2.5 acres (1 ha) Completion 2003

Interior designer Victoria Hagan Interiors Landscape architect W Garett Carlson

Photography Lars Fraser

These pages On the exterior Bryant used a slate roof, handmade bricks and a Connecticut stone base to naturally blend the house with the meticulous landscaping. This also served to treat the exterior finishes as an integral part of the paved terraces, walkways and patios. To a complement of bowed windows and box bays, adorned by shaped corbels and brackets, Bryant connected a series of trellises and pergolas that further connected the buildings with the landscaping. The custom windows were all single-glazed casement sashes with handsomely trimmed mullions, delicate muntins and grill patterns that were sized to relate to each other, but also individually scaled to each specific location.

305

These pages Bryant established a series of large-shaped ceilings, and relaxed wood paneling that became a common theme that unified the interiors of the main house and the outbuildings. The main house was to be fairly large, but Bryant used the texture, rhythm and shadow lines of the extensive painted custom millwork to create warm intimate spaces within the inter-connected open floor plan, as seen here throughout, clockwise from top left: stair hall and landing; attic stair hall; master bedroom; master bathroom; living room facing exterior; breakfast room; kitchen; living room facing interior; land stair hall (detail).

Opposite (top) The existing landscaping was to be respected as much as possible, with a concentrated effort to keep the many mature specimen trees. (bottom) Details of the updated tennis court and adjacent gable patio. Above The mood was to be relaxed, but elegant, the detailing well thought out, but based on a straightforward and familiar East Coast vocabulary with an aesthetic of planked walls, painted white clapboard siding, and decorative beams, corbels and pergolas; here is a family of custom-designed exterior light fixtures, with just the right quality of detailing and finishes, balances the rest of the exterior treatments.

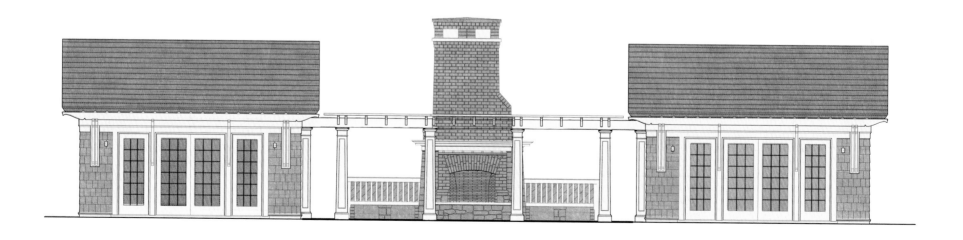

Opposite (top) Exterior view of the pool and poolhouse. **(bottom)** Elevation diagram of the pool house. **This page** Interior views of the pool house.

A Park Avenue Apartment

New York City, New York

Timothy Bryant's restoration and renovation of this Park Avenue residence re-imagined the 1917 apartment as an elegant pre-war home. Wren-period Georgian profiles and James Gibbs–inspired cornices convey a loosely 1930s feel, made all the more authentic by the revised layout's traditional division of formal and private areas, with the foyer as the central circulation area—as original architect J.E.R. Carpenter intended.

From the refinished original Cuban mahogany floors to the restored steel windows, and subtly distressed Georgian dining table, a love of old things is evident throughout. Nonetheless, the apartment is thoroughly equipped for the modern day, with closets, TVs and other amenities tucked behind hidden closets, doors, reversible bookcases, and even a framed painting in the living room.

Design is in the details. A rhythm of wall planking provides a sense of continuity between the main living spaces, while unique hardware pieces by Charles Edwards of England are eye-catching finishing touches. Examples of this abound, including the front door's swirl knobs, the Regency-style ebonized beehive doorknobs elsewhere, and black egg-and-dart moldings to top it off.

More than 90 years since his groundbreaking design, Carpenter's blueprint for traditional apartment living survives on Park Avenue. And now, it is timeless.

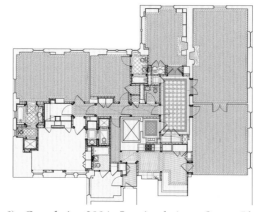

House 3800 ft² (353 m²) **Completion** 2004 **Interior designer** Owner **Photography** Simon Upton

Opposite In the entry hall, Doric entablature meets Mauch cornices, gold-leaf cove moldings and hand-printed Italian wallpaper. A floor of interlocking octagons, fabricated in water jet-cut stone, references Venice's Convento della Carita. This page To the south, the rebuilt library was handcrafted in Paris, in old-growth Oregon pine, and showcases a salvaged Georgian carved-pine mantle.

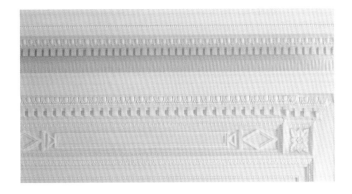

Opposite The client's remarkable art and furniture collections are front and center in every room, where ceramics, murals and rugs, and ancestral paintings are side by side with impeccably crafted new pieces. This serendipitous mix is also found in the living room, where Bryant's Corinthian entablature introduces the client's Georgian-style Scagliola mantel and an antique mirror, purchased in Ireland more than 40 years ago.

This page Against the depth and shadow of the dining room's highly embellished moldings and over doors, mid-20th-century Irish and Asian themes come together in the specially commissioned Chinese murals, Irish sideboard, ceramics, and Aubusson rug.

Above left His bathroom. Above right Her bathrom.
Left The bedroom hall.
Opposite Master bedroom.

Cory/Cornell House

Westport, Massachusetts

When Timothy Bryant started his work on the Cory House, a late-18th-century farmstead in Westport, Massachusetts, the property was slated for demolition. Its grounds were strewn with debris, its outbuildings were in complete disrepair, and the exterior planking was so damaged in some areas that vegetation grew through the walls. Little did he know that this was to become an irresistible counterpart to the fast-pace of Manhattan living as his primary residence.

With the help of a local preservation consultant, Bryant pieced together the story of the house. Tree-ring dating performed on the oak post-and-beam framing revealed that the lumber was cut in 1777. Fragments of interior millwork, recovered from a burn pile on the property, helped to accurately re-create new cornices, door casings, base boards, chair rails, sliding shutters, and mantels.

In 2004 the house received the Sarah R. Delano Preservation Award, given to individuals and organizations that have made "outstanding contributions to rehabilitation, restoration and interpretation of the historic character and environment of Greater New Bedford." A preservation award from the Massachusetts Historical Commission followed in 2007, and entry to the National Registration of Historic Places followed shortly thereafter.

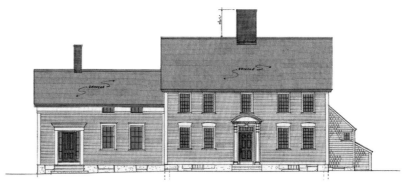

House 3000 ft² (279 m²)   **Site** 3.62 acres (1.47 ha)   **Completion** 2007
Interior designer Timothy Bryant   **Landscape and plant consultant** Edward Bowen
Historic building consultant Anne W. Baker   **Photography** Nat Rea

These pages When the faux-brick siding came off, it revealed shadow lines of the original front door surround and pediment and curved window heads, providing a blueprint for new exterior trim. Fortunately the asphalt roofing and imitation brick siding installed in the 1920s protected the original oak roof, wall planking and the oak frame, which are now once again visible in the rear façade of the house.

The property was further developed selectively with a few related, age-appropriate structures. An 1840s carriage house, moved to the site from Coventry, Rhode Island, contains chilled water units, as well as electrical, telephone and cable services; all lines run underground to the main house to avoid any panels being attached to the building. An orchard of mature apple trees was transplanted from nearby, completing the idyllic scenery.

Above Entrance hall with new kitchen and pantry beyond. Right and opposite The beehive oven was rebuilt and restored to its rightful place according to a description found in a 1796 will written by the original inhabitant, William Cory. All new work such as the small addition, kitchen and bathroom cabinetry were designed using period details from various parts of the house.

These pages A box of snapshots, taken by people who had lived in the house from the 1920s to the 1960s, was discovered in one of the outbuildings. This spectacular windfall of reference information was used to ascertain appropriate designs, colors, textures and materials for the interior spaces.

These pages The interior spaces, such as the
bathroom and main bedroom, are filled with light and
exude warmth and comfort.

Fifth Avenue Townhouse

New York City, New York

In 1899 the world-renowned architect C.P.H. Gilbert saw the completion of his design for a pair of townhouses on Fifth Avenue in his signature beaux-arts style. It remained under the ownership of the original family until 1944, and received Landmarks Designation in 1982. The current resident acquired one of the townhouses in 2008, and retained Timothy Bryant Architect to complete a historically sensitive restoration and renovation. At more than 16,000 square feet (1486 square meters), it is currently one of the 10 largest single-family residences in Manhattan, and one of only a few townhouses that survive on Fifth Avenue.

The renovation increased usable living space with a new 7th floor, basement conversion, and a modest 10-foot (3-meter) expansion of the lower two floors into the rear yard. Inside, the program is typical of contemporary single-family townhouse living, with a generous kitchen on the garden level, entertaining space on the parlor level and bedrooms above. With a swift elevator ride to the top floor, the family splits its time between the beautifully landscaped rear yard and a bright airy family room adjoining a spacious stone-paved roof terrace.

House 16,000 ft² (1486 m²)   **Site** 3670 acres (1485 ha)   **Completion** 2007

Interior designer Victoria Hagan Interiors **Landscape architects** Edmund Hollander Design

Photography Jonathan Wallen

Opposite The mansard roof's original slate tile shingles had been replaced with asphalt shingles that were failing. After careful color-matching, the roof was completely re-shingled and re-flashed with new slate tile. The dormers' existing metal roofs required complete replacement, while the original decorative copper details were scraped and re-finished, and modillions, pilasters and dentils were repaired or replaced. A specialist in paint analysis determined the color of the original decorative metal work, which had been re-painted many times over the years. All exterior brick and limestone work was cleaned, re-pointed, repaired or replaced. From the rusticated limestone garden level with decorative Roman brick above, to beaux-arts–style limestone surrounds, lintels, quoins and banding up to the roof, the entire masonry façade was meticulously restored. The splendor of the original main entry with its limestone portico, balcony, balustrade and fluted Ionic columns was still evident, but the original lower entrance and areaway were long gone. In the absence of physical or historical evidence, Bryant re-created them in accordance with existing elements and neighborhood precedents. This page World-famous landscape architect Edmund Hollander transformed the rear yard into a splendid garden. Other examples of Bryant's painstaking restoration include the copper bay window on the rear façade, which he had rebuilt with leaded glass to match the original, and his design and detailing of the rear yard's lower extension, where the size and coursing of new brick were carefully matched to those of the originals. Bryant used a classical metal frieze and crown to support the addition's roof, while collaborating with Edmund Hollander on one of his trademark traditional wood pergolas to cover the terrace against the building in the yard below.

Opposite View from the foyer. Above The renowned interior designer Victoria Hagen worked tirelessly with Bryant finding new and varied ways to complement every classical detail. Left A specialist in traditional decorative and flat plasterwork carefully researched artworks and molds from which appropriate crowns, casings, astragals and other elements were created and installed throughout the residence. These provide historical context for new stone fireplace mantels, and abundant wood-paneled walls and doors.

Following pages Bryant's sweeping five-story elliptical stair is the focal point of the new interior, and features traditional geometry and historically accurate details. The carefully researched baluster and handrail designs were custom-fabricated in bronze by a master metal worker. Bryant designed new decorative stone casings and wainscot, along with a coffered barrel-vault plaster ceiling in the entry foyer to evoke the historic original.

This page Views of the stair hall.
Opposite View of the formal dining room.

House in the Berkshires

Salisbury, Connecticut

The town of Salisbury, Connecticut, is the product of its striking surroundings. Nestled in the Berkshires, the low mountains, beautiful walking and hiking trails and views of the Twin Lakes, lend themselves to simple, vernacular architecture. On a summer trip, the client discovered a 15-acre site atop a granite outcrop where only a dilapidated lodge and the footprint of an orchard remained. Recalling the region's farming heritage, Timothy Bryant went back to basics with a new Greek Revival–inspired home that celebrates traditional craftsmanship and relates to the region's history while integrating with the surrounding landscape.

As requested by the client, the first floor accommodates both a master suite and an office with a separate entry. From its north-south axis to its interior layout, Bryant designed the house with natural daylight in mind, creating sunny spaces that are welcoming throughout the day.

From the wainscoting to the cupboards, locally built cabinetry abounds, with unique pieces of bespoke millwork evident throughout.

House 3000 ft² (279 m²) **Site** 15 acres (6 ha) **Completion** 2007
Interior designer Timothy Whealon **Landscape architect** Timothy Bryant
Photography Simon Upton

Above An unexpected double-height staircase rises from the entry hall to where the guest bedrooms on the second floor, and beyond that a cozy third floor above, overlook the site. Right View of the sumptuous living room space.

Following pages Adjacent to the entry hall, the integrated family room, kitchen and dining area is flooded with sunlight from morning to dusk, and opens to the outdoors through a screened porch. Against interior designer Timothy Whealon's soothing palette of floor and wall finishes a central fireplace unifies the space, while a blend of Swedish and English antiques creates a sense of heritage that complements the custom woodwork.

These pages A calming palette of neutral colors.

Architect Profiles

Charles Hilton Architects (page 13)
address 170 Mason Street, Greenwich, Connecticut 06830
telephone (203) 489-3800
email mail@hiltonarchitects.com
website www.hiltonarchitects.com

Franck & Lohsen Architects (page 61)
address 2233 Wisconsin Avenue NW , Suite 212, Washington D.C. 20007
telephone (202) 223-9449
email dc@francklohsen.com
website www.francklohsen.com

Hamady Architects (page 109)
address 34 E Putnam Avenue, Suite 115, Greenwich, Connecticut 06830
telephone (203) 717-1090
email kahlil@hamadyarchitectsllc.com
website www.hamadyarchitectsllc.com

John Milner Architects (page 157)
address 104 Lakeview Drive, Chadds Ford, Pennsylvania 19317
telephone (610) 388-0111
email info@johnmilnerarch.com
website www.johnmilnerarchitects.com

Ken Tate Architect (page 205)
address 433 N. Columbia Street., Suite 2, Covington, Louisiana 70433
telephone (985) 845-8181
email info@kentatearchitect.com
website www.kentatearchitect.com

Smith Architectural Group (page 253)
address 206 Phipps Plaza, Palm Beach, Florida 33480
telephone (561) 832-0202
email info@smitharchitecturalgroup.com
website www.smitharchitecturalgroup.com

Timothy Bryant Architect (page 301)
address 66 West Broadway, New York City, New York 10007
telephone (212) 571-6885
email tbryant@timothybryant.com
website www.timothybryant.com

Image Credits

Index